S0-BCK-977

THE
HISTORY OF
SINGAPORE

THE
HISTORY OF
SINGAPORE

Jean E. Abshire

The Greenwood Histories of the Modern Nations
Frank W. Thackeray and John E. Findling, Series Editors

 GREENWOOD

AN IMPRINT OF ABC-CLIO, LLC
Santa Barbara, California • Denver, Colorado • Oxford, England

Copyright 2011 by Jean E. Abshire

Library of Congress Cataloging-in-Publication Data

Abshire, Jean E.
   The history of Singapore / Jean E. Abshire.
      p. cm. — (The Greenwood histories of the modern nations)
   Includes bibliographical references and index.
   ISBN 978–0–313–37742–6 (hard copy : acid-free paper) — ISBN 978–0–313–37743–3 (ebook)
1. Singapore—History. I. Title.
DS610.4.A27   2011
959.57—dc22   2010047889

ISBN: 978–0–313–37742–6
EISBN: 978–0–313–37743–3

15 14 13 12 11   1 2 3 4 5

This book is also available on the World Wide Web as an eBook.
Visit www.abc-clio.com for details.

Greenwood
An Imprint of ABC-CLIO, LLC

ABC-CLIO, LLC
130 Cremona Drive, P.O. Box 1911
Santa Barbara, California 93116-1911

This book is printed on acid-free paper ∞

Manufactured in the United States of America

Contents

Series Foreword

The Greenwood Histories of the Modern Nations series is intended to provide students and interested laypeople with up-to-date, concise, and analytical histories of many of the nations of the contemporary world. Not since the 1960s has there been a systematic attempt to publish a series of national histories; and as series advisors, we believe that this series will prove to be a valuable contribution to our understanding of other countries in our increasingly interdependent world.

Some 40 years ago, at the end of the 1960s, the cold war was an accepted reality of global politics. The process of decolonization was still in progress, the idea of a unified Europe with a single currency was unheard of, the United States was mired in a war in Vietnam, and the economic boom in Asia was still years in the future. Richard Nixon was president of the United States, Mao Tse-tung (not yet Mao Zedong) ruled China, Leonid Brezhnev guided the Soviet Union, and Harold Wilson was prime minister of the United Kingdom. Authoritarian dictators still controlled most of Latin America, the Middle East was reeling in the wake of the Six-Day War, and Shah Mohammad Reza Pahlavi was at the height of his power in Iran.

Since then, the Cold War has ended, the Soviet Union has vanished, leaving 16 independent republics in its wake, the advent of the computer age has radically transformed global communications, the rising demand for oil makes the Middle East still a dangerous flashpoint, and the rise of new economic powers like the People's Republic of China and India threatens to bring about a new world order. All of these developments have had a dramatic impact on the recent history of every nation of the world.

For this series, which was launched in 1998, we first selected nations whose political, economic, and sociocultural affairs marked them as among the most important of our time. For each nation, we found an author who was recognized as a specialist in the history of that nation. These authors worked cooperatively with us and with Greenwood Press to produce volumes that reflected current research on their nations and that are interesting and informative to their readers. In the first decade of the series, more than 40 volumes were published; and as of 2008, some are moving into second editions.

The success of the series has encouraged us to broaden our scope to include additional nations, whose histories have had significant effects on their regions, if not on the entire world. In addition, geopolitical changes have elevated other nations into positions of greater importance in world affairs and, so, we have chosen to include them in this series as well. The importance of a series such as this cannot be underestimated. As a superpower whose influence is felt all over the world, the United States can claim a special relationship with almost every other nation. Yet many Americans know very little about the histories of nations with which the United States relates. How did they get to be the way they are? What kind of political systems have evolved there? What kind of influence do they have on their own regions? What are the dominant political, religious, and cultural forces that move their leaders? These and many other questions are answered in the volumes of this series.

The authors who contribute to this series write comprehensive histories of their nations, dating back, in some instances, to prehistoric times. Each of them, however, has devoted a significant portion of their book to events of the past 40 years because the modern era has contributed the most to contemporary issues that have an impact on U.S. policy. Authors make every effort to be as up-to-date as possible so that readers can benefit from discussion and analysis of recent events.

In addition to the historical narrative, each volume contains an introductory chapter giving an overview of that country's geography, political institutions, economic structure, and cultural attributes. This is meant to give readers a snapshot of the nation as it exists in the contemporary world. Each history also includes supplementary information following the narrative, which may include a timeline that represents a succinct chronology of the nation's historical evolution, biographical sketches of the nation's most important historical figures, and a glossary of important terms or concepts that are usually expressed in a foreign language. Finally, each author prepares a comprehensive bibliography for readers who wish to pursue the subject further.

Readers of these volumes will find them fascinating and well-written. More importantly, they will come away with a better understanding of the contemporary world and the nations that comprise it. As series advisors, we hope that this series will contribute to a heightened sense of global understanding as we move through the early years of the twenty-first century.

Frank W. Thackeray and John E. Findling
Indiana University Southeast

Acknowledgments

I would like to thank the staff at the Central Library of the National University of Singapore for granting me access to their collection, which greatly facilitated the writing of this book, and the many excellent scholars who have devoted years of effort researching and writing about this fascinating country. I am grateful to the series editors, John Findling and Frank Thackeray of Indiana University Southeast, and Kaitlin Ciarmiello of ABC-CLIO for this opportunity and for their support during the process. I appreciate the assistance of Arathi Pillai and the rest of the team at PreMediaGlobal for their assistance in the production phase. The book is better thanks to the proof-reading assistance of Brigette Adams and Jodie Beatty; any errors are my own. I am indebted to Dr. Norman Furniss of Indiana University, Bloomington for years of intellectual guidance and a deeper understanding of how to study other countries. Finally, I would like to thank my colleagues, friends, and family for their patience and encouragement during the last two years. I dedicate this book to my father, Charles Abshire, and in memory of my mother, Cleo, wonderful parents who always encouraged me to ask questions.

Timeline of Major Events

1859	Fort Canning constructed
1867	Straits Settlements became a crown colony
1869	Suez Canal opened; Singapore became a coaling station for steamships
1873	British expanded control on Malay Peninsula increasing Singapore's exports of rubber and tin
1877	Chinese Protectorate created
1903	Singapore was world's seventh largest port in tonnage
1906	Singapore Chinese Chamber of Commerce founded
1910	Colonial administration took over opium production in Singapore
1914	Indentured labor from China banned
	Sale of women and girls for prostitution banned
1915	Mutiny of Indian soldiers stationed in Singapore
1921	Britain decided to build naval station in Singapore
1929	Great Depression harmed Singapore's trade
1931, 1933	Laws passed limiting immigration from China
1938	Sembawang Naval Base opened
1939	World War II began in Europe
July 1941	Vichy France gave Japan access to airbases in Indochina
	United States froze Japanese assets
	Japan made final decision to invade Singapore via the Malay Peninsula
December 8, 1941	Japan bombed Singapore, launched attack down Malay Peninsula
January 31, 1942	British and Commonwealth forces retreated to Singapore
February 8, 1942	Japanese forces launched attach on Singapore
February 15, 1942	Britain surrendered Singapore to Japan
February 18, 1942	*Sook ching* process against the Chinese community began
August 15, 1945	Emperor Hirohito officially announced Japan's surrender

September 2, 1945	British and Commonwealth forces landed in Singapore
1947	Singapore's trade reached prewar levels
1948–1960	State of emergency
1950–1953	Korean War fueled economic boom
1954–1964	Singapore shaken by waves of communist political violence
1954	Rendel Commission recommended constitutional reforms
1955	People's Action Party founded
	David Marshall elected first chief minister of Singapore
	Lee Hock Bus Strike
1959	New constitutional arrangements gave self-governance on most issues
1960	Singapore was world's largest exporter of rubber
1961	Singapore Economic Development Board founded
1963–1966	Undeclared war with Indonesia (*Konfrontasi*)
1963	Merger with Malaysia
1964	Ethnic riots shook Singapore
1965	Singapore declared independence
1967	Association of Southeast Asian Nations (ASEAN) founded
1967–1968	Major reforms set foundation for rapid economic growth
1968	British announced withdrawal from Singaporean military bases within three years
1973	Singapore had world's third largest oil refining facilities
1975	Singapore was world's third largest port
	Singapore achieved zero population growth
1976	Government announced the Second Industrial Revolution
1978	China's Deng Xiaoping visited Singapore

1979	Speak Mandarin Campaign launched
1981	PAP lost first parliamentary seat since 1966 to an opposition party
1985	GDP and per capita income fell for first time since independence
1986	Government announced new economic development program
1989	Housing Development Board had built 835,000 apartments since 1960
1990	Port of Singapore achieved status of world's busiest port
	Lee Kwan Yew stepped down; Goh Chok Tong became prime minister
	All political dissidents released from detention
1991	Shared Values Campaign began
1994	American teenager Michael Fay caned for vandalism
1997	Asian economic crisis put Singapore into second recession
2001	Economy returned to recession
	New economic development plan introduced
2001–2002	Islamic terrorists arrested in Singapore
2003	SARS outbreak
2004	Lee Hsien Loong became third prime minister
2007	Government announced plan to become an international education and medical tourism hub
2008–2009	Recession from global financial crisis
2010	IMF predicted an 8.9 percent 2010 growth rate for Singapore

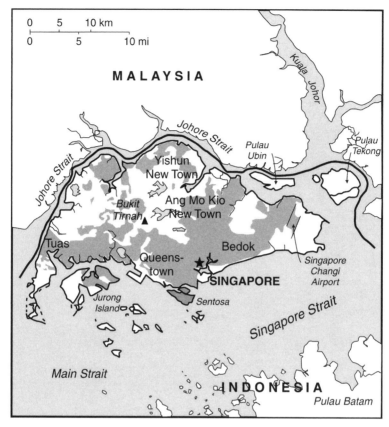

Map of Singapore. (Courtesy of Bookcomp)

1

A Globalized City-State

Imagine a poverty-stricken country with people living packed together in a slum along a river that doubles as a sewer. Now fast-forward just a couple of decades and envision tourist boats on a river against a backdrop of glass-faced skyscrapers sparkling in the tropical sun. This is the journey of Singapore, from third world to first world. Many people think immediately of China or India when they think of rapid economic development through globalization, but Singapore succeeded in moving from third world to first almost before China even entered the race—and Singapore has come farther. One of the Asian Tigers, together with Hong Kong, South Korea, and Taiwan, these economies became famous for their high economic growth rates and rapid industrialization from the 1960s onward. They achieved this through intensive participation in the global economy.

Many Westerners may think of harsh government practices or strict societal order when they think of Singapore. This is due to high profile events such as the 1994 caning (whipping with a flexible rattan cane) of American teenager Michael Fay for vandalism, references in the media to the fact that littering and chewing gum sales are illegal, and that drinking or eating in the subway can merit a several-hundred-dollar fine.

However, when Singaporeans think of what it means to be Singaporean, for many the national image is a globalized city-state, as embodied by the slogan "Global City, World of Opportunities" used by Singapore 2006, a major event launching the first Singapore Biennale. However, slogans do not begin to capture the essence of this fascinating, colorful, diverse, and globalized country. A slogan does not show the vivid yellow and magenta blooms of the flower stalls in the Little India neighborhood or tickle one's nose with the incense drifting from the Buddhist temple down the street. It does not begin to depict the towering skyscrapers of the Central Business District that are filled with the names of corporations from all around the globe or the heat, noise, hustle, and smells of a hawker center food court. During the lunch rush people savor Chinese, Malay, Indian, Indonesian, European, or Japanese dishes reflecting the amazing social diversity that is Singapore, a diversity that comes through Singapore's position at the leading edge of globalization.

At 269 square miles (just about three and a half times the size of Washington, D.C.), Singapore is one of the smallest countries in the world when measured by territory and has only 4.7 million people; yet in terms of economics, it is a powerhouse with a 2009 gross domestic product (GDP) ranking of 48 out of 227 countries.[1] When analyzed on a per capita basis, Singapore's GDP status is even more impressive: seventh in the world behind Lichtenstein, Qatar, Luxembourg, Bermuda, Norway, and Kuwait.[2] This is amazing wealth for a country that in the 1960s was considered to be among the poorest, a part of the less developed world. One might ask how Singapore accomplished this. The short answer is globalization, defined as the increasing economic, social, and political integration of countries and peoples. In 2009, Singapore ranked first in the world for having the most globalized economy and seventh in the world for social globalization.[3]

Globalization has been one of the strongest forces shaping Singapore throughout its history. Its geographic location at the tip of the Malay Peninsula in Southeast Asia, just a little over a 100 miles north of the equator, placed it at a crossroads for trade, first regional, then global. Almost everything about Singapore, from its people to its languages and cuisine to its businesses and even its political history, has been inseparable from globalization.

New York Times journalist Thomas Friedman wrote *The World Is Flat*, a book in which he described globalization as having different phases, Globalization 1.0, 2.0, and 3.0. Globalization 1.0 was the integration brought by European colonization. Wealthy countries and their governments drove this phase of globalization as they sought territory and wealth to expand their power. Globalization 2.0 came later when multinational corporations began to drive global integration. This phase began with the advent of corporations like the British East India Company, which profoundly shaped Singapore for four crucial decades in its history. The multinational corporations found motivation in their search for markets, labor, and profits. While interrupted by events such as World Wars I and II, corporate globalization was the primary force in the world from 1800 until 2000. Globalization 3.0 is, according to Friedman, a variation in which people are the driving force, empowered by technology like the Internet to reach around the globe. So where does Singapore fit into this? Singapore *is* globalization. It was a global crossroads, a place where boundaries were broken down through trade for hundreds of years before the Europeans arrived to expand their imperial hold. It was later controlled by Britain in the name of corporate globalization and is an outstanding example of Globalization 2.0. After it gained independence in 1965, Singapore learned to harness globalization, to become a center of global trade, finance, shipping, and technology of a greater caliber than it had been under British colonial control. With this harnessing of globalization, Singapore expanded its wealth and its prominence. Thus, globalization is the underlying theme for this examination of Singapore's rich history. Its small size has not left it on the sidelines. Its geographic position has lent itself to trade and given Singapore a status across the centuries that is uncommon for such a diminutive territory.

PEOPLE

Singapore's population was formed by globalization, as people came from other areas to engage in trade or work in trade-related businesses and industry in an economically vibrant location. Singapore's current population is predominantly (77%) of Chinese origin. This group, however, also exhibits diversity, as the forebearers came from different parts of China, bringing with them different dialects, foods, and traditions. Today, the largest subgroup is Hokkien-speakers descended from immigrants from the Fujian Province; the next largest is Teochew-speakers, whose origins are in the northeastern part of Guandong Province; and finally those speaking the Yue (Cantonese) dialect who are descended from the Guangzhou area of the Guandong Province. The next largest ethnic group at 14 percent is the indigenous people of the region, the Malays.[4] While the Malays may have been the original inhabitants, the Chinese quickly outnumbered them. The next largest ethnic group is Indian at 8 percent, who, like the Chinese, came from different parts of India for economic opportunity and, thus, are diverse within their community as well, although approximately two-thirds are from Tamil areas in southern India and northern Sri Lanka. The next two largest groups, each comprising about 8 percent of the Indian community are Punjabis from Punjab in northern India and Malayalis from Kerala State.[5]

The demographic composition is reflected in Singapore's four official languages of Chinese, English, Malay, and Tamil. Each of these is widely spoken, with most people speaking at least two languages. English, however, is the common language of business, government, and increasingly everyday life. Unofficially, there is a Singaporean Creole language, known as Singlish. It is English-based with the addition of some Malay and Hokkien words and grammar. The government frowns on the language, declaring it incompatible with Singapore's image as a serious business center, and even began a Speak Good English Movement to discourage the use of Singlish. Despite these efforts, it remains very popular in television shows and local films, although one (a comedy) received an adult rating in 2002 for containing "excessive Singlish."

Singapore's immigrants also brought considerable religious diversity. Buddhism and Taoism are most prevalent in the Chinese community; Islam is the religion of almost everyone in the Malay community and some in the Indian community; Hinduism is the most widely practiced faith among Singaporean Indians; and a range of Christian denominations are practiced by some Chinese and Indians. In recent years Islam has come to be treated with caution due to the rising threat from Islamic terrorism. Instead of cracking down on religious practice, however, the government has worked with the Muslim community to encourage religious harmony and to encourage the Muslim community itself to limit extremism in religious education.

Despite the diversity within society, there is evidence that Singapore is developing a common national identity, that people increasingly identify themselves as Singaporean, rather than by their communal group. This development was long hindered by the fact that immigrants typically did not come to Singapore with the intention of staying. Instead, they intended to work for a time and then return home, thus retaining strong connections with their homeland. Later, leaders planned for Singapore to merge with neighboring Malaysia, so many people never expected Singapore to become an independent country until it actually happened. It has taken time to overcome this history and the societal divisions that separated the ethnic groups. The Singaporean national identity is not a finished product, but it is emerging. The goal of the government after independence was expressed by Foreign Minister Sinnathamby Rajaratnam, who thought that Singaporeans would be people "rooted in the cultures of four great civilizations but not belonging exclusively to any of them."[6] Despite that, however, marriage rates between members of the different ethnic communities are quite low; and even with government programs to integrate housing, the communities have somewhat resegregated in recent decades.

While Singapore has considerable diversity among its citizens, that is only part of the story. The reality of globalization in Singapore is that the country continues to draw people from around the world for work and economic benefits. Singapore ranks fifteenth in the world for migration into the country, thus Singapore's diversity continues to evolve.[7] In fact, the 2000 census revealed that close to 20 percent of the residents were non-citizens.[8] Singapore's openness to the world's peoples is likely to continue, since the government sees immigration as central to the country's ongoing economic growth and the mitigation of Singapore's alarmingly low birthrate. Thus, Singapore is and will be a global city-state.

GOVERNMENT

Singapore's government is a parliamentary republic with a single legislative body of 84 elected seats and up to nine appointed seats intended to offer non-partisan voices in the parliament. The leader of the strongest party in the Parliament is the prime minister, who with the cabinet and the president comprises the executive branch. The presidency was for decades a ceremonial role, but in 1991, the powers of the office were expanded by constitutional amendment. It became an elected position and the president gained veto power over some financial matters, such as spending the national reserves, and also over appointment to some official positions, including civil service and government companies. These powers, however, are limited, and the real power within the government rests with the prime minister.

While those are the constitutional arrangements, the dynamics of political power play out somewhat differently due to Singapore's party politics. Although a variety of political parties exist, there is only one, the People's Action Party (PAP), that exercises power and has done so with very little competition since 1959, even before Singapore gained independence. The PAP controlled 100 percent of the seats in the Parliament from 1966, when members of the opposition Barisan Sosialis party resigned, until 1981, when one seat was lost to a Workers' Party member in a special election. Following the next general election in 1984, the government enacted a new policy to guarantee the opposition parties at least three seats in parliament, even if they won fewer than three, so there could be at least some assurance of opposition representation. However, since 1988, the government has formed increasing numbers of "group representation constituencies" (multiple representatives for each voting district) in place of a single elected official representing a voting district. This group system involves voting for parties rather than candidates, and the party that wins the largest number of votes wins all the seats allotted to the electoral district. This was introduced to improve minority representation in the parliament since a certain level of minority representation is required in the electoral groups, but there are allegations that this system has made it more difficult for opposition parties to compete in elections. Indeed, in the last several elections, there have been just two elected opposition members of parliament, and thus far no opposition party has won a group representation constituency. The PAP's control of Parliament, and thus of the executive branch, is exceedingly strong and gives the party almost unlimited political power in Singapore.

The PAP also manages to dominate nongovernmental aspects of the political system. Most community organizations are in some way affiliated with the party. There are strict controls on local and international media organizations. For instance, the *Wall Street Journal Asia* and other organizations have been sued by government officials for libel and defamation. The expansion of the internet poses opportunities for greater freedom of speech, conforming to Friedman's idea of Globalization 3.0, but the Singaporean government has been a leader among restrictive countries in limiting the ability of citizens to use the Internet for opposition. Any Web site with "political intent" must be registered with the government and several have closed down under government pressure. At the same time, the administration has been an innovator in using the Internet to make the government more accessible to its citizens. The government portal, eCitizen, is a one-stop connection for most government services. If someone needs a pet license, eCitizen will provide the form, along with links to lists of veterinarians, information on pet shops and animal welfare organizations, and education for pet owners. If someone wants to get married, eCitizen offers links to "find your soulmate," registration information for civil or Muslim marriages, and advice to keep the marriage happy, such as dealing with in-laws, financial management, communication, parenthood, etc. This selective approach to political globalization is the single weak point (albeit an important one) in Singapore's status as a globalization leader.

ECONOMY

Singapore has, as indicated above, a robust, capitalist economy. Manufacturing and financial services are the most significant sectors, with export of consumer electronics, computer products, and pharmaceuticals leading the way. The United States, Malaysia, China, Hong Kong, Japan, and Indonesia are Singapore's most significant trading partners. Like most advanced economies, it is heavily vested in services (73%), with industry comprising only 27 percent of GDP. Although Singapore's wealth is enormous, it is not evenly distributed across members of the society. Singapore ranks twenty-ninth worst in the world for income inequality,[9] despite having the second highest standard of living in Asia, behind Japan.[10]

While Singapore has one of the most open economies in the world, it is not an economy in which government is uninvolved. Indeed, one factor that makes Singapore an inviting location for investment is the high degree of stability afforded by the consistency and control of government. The architect of Singapore's economic development strategy, Finance Minister Goh Keng Swee, argued that "The role of government is pivotal. Non-economic factors . . . are more important than economic variables."[11] Singaporean economist Tilak Abeysinghe refers to it as a "market driven guided economy," in which the government has a heavy presence through statutory boards, land ownership, government holding companies, and government-linked companies. One of the most noteworthy aspects of the government's management of the economy is its agile efforts to keep up with global market leaders. Again and again, as global markets changed, Singapore's policy-makers shifted economic priorities to keep Singapore competitive and its services marketable. Often this involved financial incentives to businesses and major retraining programs for the population. Recently, the government has targeted new areas for expanding Singapore's participation in the knowledge-based economy, focusing on medical tourism because excellent medical care is much less expensive than in the United States and focusing on becoming an "education hub" for the world, seeking to capitalize on its recent investments in improving higher education by inviting international students to study in Singapore. Another new and controversial economic undertaking, expected to bring in billions of dollars per year by 2015, is casino gambling as part of two integrated resort projects that the government hopes will boost tourism.

SOCIETY AND CULTURE

For most of the country's existence, Singapore's people were self-segregated into ethnic neighborhoods like Chinatown, Kampong Glam for the Malay population, and Little India. The Chinese and Indians lived in the most urban environments, and many Malays lived in more rural, traditional villages. As the government began to improve housing in the 1960s, this aspect of society was transformed. Today, almost everyone lives in apartment housing, most of it ethnically integrated, and most own their own apartments. Most of the apartments are in high-rise buildings, as Singapore's population density is among the highest in the world.

With this improvement in housing, came improvements in infrastructure. The government invested heavily in a Mass Rapid Transit (MRT) system, which opened in 1987, involving a combination of subway and above-ground trains that move people around the island and among the new neighborhoods that developed with the housing construction. The government has sought to limit the number of automobiles to save Singapore from the problems of traffic congestion that plague many major cities by requiring a Certificate of Entitlement in order to purchase a car. People must bid on the limited number of available certificates and pay high fees (such as a 41% tax to import a car), which makes vehicle ownership prohibitive for most Singaporeans. Public transit is the most accessible means of transportation for nearly everyone. Other social improvements include nearly 100 percent literacy, a healthy population, and a life expectancy that rivals other wealthy countries. Political leaders viewed these improvements as necessary for economic development; the country needed healthy, educated workers with an infrastructure able to support participation in the global economy.

Due to the lack of land and the country's rush to build office towers to house its expanding business operations, most of the traditional appearances of Singapore vanished decades ago, as older buildings were razed after people resettled in improved housing. In the 1980s, a limited conservation effort began and some "godowns" (warehouses) along the Singapore River were preserved and converted into restaurants, nightclubs, and other tourist attractions, and several other neighborhoods, including the previously mentioned Chinatown, Kampong Glam, and Little India, benefited from efforts to save some of the old "shophouses," a distinctive Singaporean form of architecture that combined businesses on the lower levels with living and storage space on the upper levels.

In terms of culture, Singaporeans are hard working with a five-and-a-half-day workweek (44 hours) being the norm. After work, people tend to pursue two favorite activities, shopping and eating. As the tourism industry expanded from the mid-1970s, large shopping complexes were developed, leaving Singaporeans, as well as their visitors, with almost unlimited shopping opportunities. The love of shopping is so common that even Prime Minister Goh Chok Tong commented that people's lives would not be complete without it.

Singapore is also known as a "foodie nation," with a high level of general interest in anything related to food and eating. While there are restaurants of many kinds, most Singaporeans eat at hawker centers. Prior to the development of improved housing, average people often did not have cooking facilities in the small accommodations they typically shared with other workers. To meet their need for food, the practice of hawking developed, with people selling prepared food from the streets. A hawker would typically specialize in just a couple of dishes, reflecting of his culture of origin. As the Singaporean government began to intervene in daily activities to improve public health, it quickly turned to the sometimes unhygienic practices of the hawkers. The government chose to ban street hawking, and instead created countless hawker centers where the hawkers could sell their goods from stalls with proper sanitation facilities in open-air food courts. The hawker centers are an institution, with most Singaporeans eating at least one meal a day in a hawker center, and oftentimes more. The stalls in the hawker centers sell dishes from each of the ethnic communities and, as globalization increased, so too did the array of hawker center options, which today may include British fish and chips, American hamburgers and fries, Japanese udon noodles, French pastries, etc. There is typically at least one hawker center in each housing development, and they are also scattered around the central business district, so most people live their lives only a short walk from a rich array of affordable foods. Many hawkers still specialize in just a few items, and sometimes they use recipes that have been handed down through generations of hawker families. The hawker culture is taken seriously enough that Singapore's premier dining guide, *Makansutra*, includes hawker stalls in its rankings, with some hawkers gaining the publication's highest rating of "die die must try!"

This cultural focus on shopping and eating, along with the government's belief that a global city-state should have certain amenities, may have created concern among some public officials that Singapore lacked adequate high culture. Thus, in recent years, Singapore has invested greatly in the arts. The most obvious indicator of this is the new performing arts center, Esplanade—Theatres on the Bay, which features performers from around the world. There is a month-long

Singapore Arts Festival, which is the country's largest annual cultural event. There is also encouragement for a local arts scene, but some artists feel constrained by the censorship of Singapore's "out-of-bounds markers," which are topics that, in the eyes of the government, are too sensitive for public discussion, including race relations, religion, and politics. The government invested in museums, including the Asian Civilizations Museum with an extensive art collection, and Cultural Heritage Centers reflecting each of the ethnic communities.

Overall, Singapore is a conservative country. The government has a large role in shaping public and even private life with the expectations of proper behavior and decorum. It strictly prohibits pornography; even *Cosmopolitan* magazine was banned until the 1990s. Homosexual activities are still criminal, although there are increasing public, and even government, discussions questioning the policy. Promiscuity of any sort is unwelcome. Alcoholic beverages taxes are extremely high to discourage alcohol consumption. Drug traffickers, such as people possessing more than a half an ounce of heroin or an ounce of cocaine, are subject to public hanging. Some elected officials found distasteful the government's recent decision to create casino gambling, and the issue unleashed furious public debates as it drew opposition from many in society. Government rhetoric often contrasts Singaporean values with those of the selfish, decadent West, where crime, divorce, drug use, and other social problems are portrayed as rampant and adds to cautionary tales about such developments not being welcome in Singapore. Leaders heavily promote family values that help maintain the conservative orientation of society. In this respect, Singapore is being shielded from some aspects of cultural globalization, although there are pressures pushing at those limits.

If globalization is considered to be increasing interaction and decreasing barriers among different peoples, economies, and political systems, the following chapters make evident that Singapore has experienced these forces since the beginning. Initially, it was a small port in a mostly regional trade network of Southeast Asia, with some connections extending as far as China and the Middle East. It came under the influence of different regional kingdoms or sultanates, as different empires rose and fell. Once Europeans began colonizing the region, Singapore and its affiliated sultanates struggled to cope with this new challenge and eventually came under the authority of the British trading empire, the English East India Company. Some decades later, the British Crown assumed direct control, although Singapore's role in Britain's global trading network changed little. Globalization was interrupted by World War II and Singapore's role shifted, in part, from a trading port to the bastion of defense for Britain's colonial interests in the Asia-Pacific. The war proved to be one of the most painful episodes of Singapore's history as the people suffered greatly under Japanese occupation. After the war, Singapore moved slowly toward independence and local political leaders, gradually gaining governing authority from the British Crown, set Singapore's course for the future. They recognized that a tiny island with no natural resources and a small population had to fully exploit the few resources it possessed: a strategic position at a global crossroads of trade and a hardworking citizenry. These were the factors that facilitated Singapore's rise to one of the wealthiest countries in the world. Globalization has been at the center of this—and appears to be set to continue shaping Singapore into the future.

NOTES

1. Central Intelligence Agency, "The World Factbook: Country Comparisons-GDP (Purchasing Power Parity)," Central Intelligence Agency, https://www.cia.gov/library/publications/the-world-factbook/rankorder/2001rank.html.

2. Central Intelligence Agency, "The World Factbook: Country Comparisons-GDP-per capita (PPP)," Central Intelligence Agency, https://www.cia.gov/library/publications/the-world-factbook/rankorder/2004rank.html.

3. Axel Dreher, "KOF Index of Globalization," Swiss Federal Institute of Technology Zurich, http://globalization.kof.ethz.ch/.

4. Federal Research Division, "Country Profile: Singapore," Library of Congress, http://memory.loc.gov/frd/cs/profiles/Singapore.pdf.

5. Zafar Anjum, "Indians Roar in the Lion City," *Little India*, November 12, 2005, http://www.littleindia.com/news/123/ARTICLE/1267/2005-11-12.html.

6. C. M. Turnbull, *A History of Singapore, 1819–1988,* 2nd ed. (New York: Oxford University Press, 1989), 292.

7. Central Intelligence Agency, "The World Factbook: Singapore," Central Intelligence Agency, https://www.cia.gov/library/publications/the-world-factbook/geos/sn.html.

8. Brenda S. A. Yeoh, "Singapore: Hungry for Foreign Workers at All Skill Levels," Migration Information Source, http://www.migrationinformation.org/Profiles/display.cfm?ID=570.

9. Central Intelligence Agency, "The World Factbook: Singapore," Central Intelligence Agency, https://www.cia.gov/library/publications/the-world-factbook/geos/sn.html.

10. Federal Research Division, "Country Profile: Singapore," Library of Congress, http://memory.loc.gov/frd/cs/profiles/Singapore.pdf.

11. Quoted in Tilak Abeysinghe, "Singapore: Economy," in *The Far East and Australasia*, 39th ed., edited by Lynn Daniel (London: Europa Publications, Routledge, 2008), http://courses.nus.edu.sg/course/ecstabey/Singapore%20Economy-Tilak.pdf.

2

Pre-Colonial Singapore: Temasek, Dragon's Tooth Gate, and Singapura, 100–1819

The early history of Singapore has very limited documentation. What is known is pieced together from various sources, including legend, a semi-historical document known as the *Malay Annals*, archeological evidence, records from early Chinese traders, and later documents from European colonial seafarers. It is only after Singapore became a British holding that the historical record becomes clearer. However, the evidence that exists makes it clear that human inhabitation of Singapore started centuries earlier. Its early existence and its position then was a function of what has shaped Singapore throughout its history and indeed still today: Singapore's geographic position at a cross-roads for trade and the resulting struggles between different regional and global powers to advance their positions through Singapore. Indeed, globalization informed Singapore's entire existence from its earliest days to the present, first in its advantageous position along the Maritime Silk Road, a major oceanic trade route dating back to the first millennium between East and Southeast Asia, India, the Middle East, and eventually Europe, what many scholars consider to be an early form of globalization to the intense international interconnectedness that has made Singapore the global city-state that it is today.

The early history of Singapore is, in essence, a regional history, pieced together from a variety of sources of varying degrees of accuracy and credibility. For example, a portion of the historical account is based on the *Malay Annals*, a history of the Malay nobility with roots in Singapore that was written on the command of Malay Sultan Mahmud Shah in the fifteenth century and prior to that was preserved via oral tradition, with storytellers passing the history of the community from one generation to the next. What one sees in reading the *Malay Annals* is a semi-mythological history rather than a literal account. The *Annals* were intended to be a record of the descent of the rulers, along with court customs and ceremonies, at a time when Malay control of the region was facing challenge by European colonial incursion. Probably motivated by an effort to aggrandize their past leaders, even to the point of suggesting a divine heritage, storytellers gave, in some cases, superhuman accounts of events and people. While it would be easy to dismiss such accounts, various aspects of the tales are corroborated by credible sources so these stories merit at least some consideration.

SRIVIJAYAN EMPIRE, 100–1000 C.E.

The context for the settlement of Singapore has its roots in the advantageous position and role eked out by the Srivijayan Empire, which was prominent in the region for most of the first millennium. Power and influence in the region at that time were based less on control of land, as one typically sees as a mark of power, but rather control of and access to people. A ruler with greater human resources was able to grow food, create various products, and engage in other activities that provided wealth and status. Because of this focus on human resources, conflicts between groups and approaches to protecting resources were different than one would find in a land-focused society. Land was plentiful, but people were not; so rather than fighting to defend land, leaders were much more likely to simply move their people if they came under pressure or attack from a rival group. It was much easier to create a new settlement and to clear more land for farming than to find new groups of people to become workers. Thus, cities and other population centers were much less fixed than in other parts of the world, such as ancient Greece, Egypt,

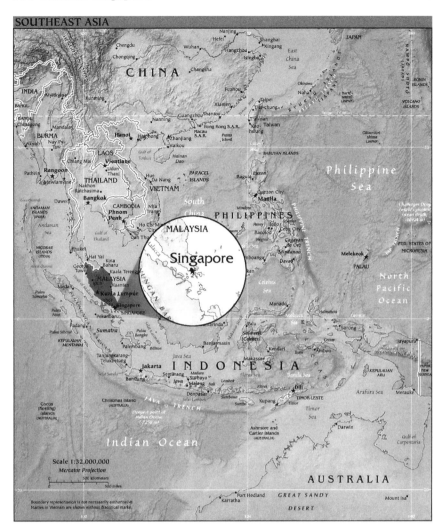

Map showing Southeast Asia. Singapore is located at the southern tip of the Malay Peninsula. (Adapted from *The World Factbook 2009*. Washington, D.C.: Central Intelligence Agency, 2009. https://www.cia.gov/library/publications/the-world-factbook/index.html)

Mesopotamia, or China. There are few fixed monuments or defensive structures for archeologists to study because the population of Southeast Asia was too transient.

The primary activity for accumulating wealth and power was control of trade, which the geography in Southeast Asia made very easy. Trade between China and India transited through the various archipelagos that comprise Southeast Asia, with one of the most strategic bottlenecks for controlling trade being the Strait of Melaka, the southern entry to which lies about 18 miles west of Singapore. The Srivijayan Empire, which lasted from 100 to 1000 C.E., established control over much of this area and its critical trade routes. The Empire's capital was at Palembang on the island of Sumatra in Indonesia and this served as the Empire's primary base for centuries, although there is also some evidence from Chinese traders that another administrative center existed farther to the north. Between these two centers, the Srivijayan leaders controlled shipping, significantly aided by their control of local peoples, particularly the *Orang Laut* (Malay for sea people), expert seamen who provided a military-like force for the leaders.

Ships had to traverse these waters for trade, but the region was known as a dangerous place because of vicious pirate attacks, including attacks by the *Orang Laut*. The *Orang Laut* would sometimes trade, but often would surround ships in hundreds of small boats and attack for days. If the winds were favorable, the ships could sometimes escape but often not. The problem was so severe that some traders resorted to avoiding the Strait of Melaka and instead offloading goods from ships, transporting the goods overland across a narrow part of the Malay Peninsula, and then reloading them on another ship to continue on to India or China. This, however, was slow and inefficient compared to simply sailing a single ship around the Malay Peninsula through the Strait of Melaka. The Srivijayan leaders coopted some of the *Orang Laut* groups, turning them into followers and their boats into something of a naval fleet. This controlled the piracy problem to a sufficient degree so that sailing through the Strait of Melaka became the preferred route for the maritime trade.

With the support of the *Orang Laut*, Srivijayan leaders forced ships sailing between China and India to stop at the Srivijayan ports where captains were forced to pay duties, thereby increasing the wealth of the Empire. Archeological evidence suggests *Orang Laut* activity on Karimun Island, located west of Singapore in the middle of the southern mouth of the Strait. This activity is noteworthy, as it would be difficult to enter or exit the Strait without being noticed from a cliff-top position on the island. A later Chinese writer noted that if a ship did not stop at the required port, it might be set on by an armed group, presumably the *Orang Laut*, and the crew would be killed. Thus, the motivation to visit Srivijayan ports and pay their duties was high.

There is some evidence of diplomatic significance of Singapore, known as Temasek, in the seventh century, primarily as a meeting point of traders, rather than as a port. There is a tale that a Srivijanan ruler, Chulan, had become angered with the emperor of China and was planning an attack. Hearing of this, the Chinese emperor sent a ship of old men and trees to meet the Srivijayan ruler. The Chinese sailors told Chulan that they had been underway since they were young men and the trees had grown from seedlings and they had grown old during the very long voyage. Deciding that China was too distant to attack, Chulan gave up. Supposedly, this meeting took place where ships from India and China would regularly meet, at Temasek.

The Srivijayan Empire was at a point of great prosperity and power when, in 1025, disaster struck. A group from the Chola kingdom in southern India launched a raid and kidnapped the Srivijayan leader. No one heard from him again, and he presumably died in captivity. This event marked the demise of the Empire and a sharp turn for the control of the trade route. For the next century, Tamil trading companies from southern India dominated the Straits region, although the domination was weaker than the control of the Srivijayan Empire. With time, the regional trading center shifted from the old Srivijayan capital of Palambang to another trade center on the island of Sumatra, Jambi, which was the center of another kingdom, Malayu. The rise of this group of traders set some developments in motion that would eventually have significant impacts on Singapore and the region.

In particular, the Malayu had a history of engagement with China, even before the rise of Srivijaya, primarily in the areas of trade and diplomacy, and thus there was a well-established connection with China in the region. About the same time as south Indian influence waned, domestic concerns in China created a context in which the connection with the Malayu would become more important. China in the Song Dynasty came under significant pressure from the Mongols to the degree that the northern Song capital fell in 1126 and was relocated southward, creating a more prominent role in the empire for the southern Chinese. The Mongol pressure continued and Chinese leaders, motivated by the desire for better trade routes and for money to fund their defensive efforts, relaxed existing rules that restricted contact between Chinese citizens and foreigners. This made it much easier for people from southern China to initiate trade voyages resulting in settlements of Chinese people in the area of the Strait of Melaka.

The development of Chinese trade settlements in the region had several lasting effects. First, as previously noted, the earlier norm was to relocate settlements as political fortunes and strategic pressures changed, but the Chinese settlements had loyalties to leaders who were not local, thus shifting that historical dynamic. Moreover, the loyalties of the Chinese merchants to a more distant major power left them less vulnerable to the manipulations of local leaders and, thus, the very restrictive port-usage requirements that led to accumulated wealth and power for the Srivijayan Empire could not be replicated. This led to the proliferation of larger numbers of ports, rather than just a couple of monopolistic ports.

ANCIENT SINGAPORE, 1299–1398

The rise of Singapore's early prominence came in the late 1200s. The history of the establishment of Singapore as an important center is problematic in its details, as the mythicized history of the *Malay Annals* is the basis for accounts of its founding, the succession of leaders, and its decline. The legend claims that there was a prince, Sang Nila Utama, who was perhaps the product of a union between an adventurer king and the princess of an underwater kingdom or a descendant of a union of Alexander the Great with an Indian princess. In a mythical story, the prince and his two brothers were each given territory, and Sang Nila Utama became rajah of Palembang. Palembang became prosperous under Sang Nila Utama's rule, but he had inherited his father's adventurous nature and decided to set out on a voyage to seek a location to found a new city.

First he went to Bintan, an island just southeast of Singapore, where the queen, Sakidar Shah, took a liking to him, adopted him, and named him her successor. Sang Nila Utama's time with the queen is significant, as she is allegedly the source of musical instruments that became tokens of nobility for later Malay rulers. That she was from Bintan Island likewise gave Bintan special significance in the following centuries. However, Sang Nila Utama again became bored with court life and set out again, this time to go hunting. He landed and hunted on one island, then when done, was taken by the view of an island some distance away, called Temasek. He sailed there and was disappointed to find very poor hunting, with only small animals and birds. Suddenly, a huge animal appeared and then disappeared again. His ministers informed him of an ancient lion that had a similar appearance. He decided that location would be a good one to establish his new city; and he named the location Singapura, or lion town, in honor of the lion. Sang Nila Utama set up his kingdom there, and what today is known as Fort Canning Hill became the royal residence. Sang Nila Utama was also known as Sri Tri Buana, a name which indicates he was ruler of three lands, probably Java, Sumatra, and Temasek. The oral record indicates that Sri Tri Buana, along with his ministers, was buried on the hill near the residence.

The *Malay Annals* do not include dates, but tracing the succession of Sang Nila Utama's descendents and dates surrounding events during their reigns suggests the establishment of the new settlement took place in 1299. The next four descendents of Sang Nila Utama maintained their base at Singapore until misfortune befell the last of them, and the capital at Singapore was abandoned in the 1390s.

It is clear from the archeological record, however, that Singapore was an important place during that century of noble presence. Uniquely, these early Singaporeans constructed a wall of significant size; scholars have found no evidence of similar structures elsewhere in the region. While there is no clear evidence of the original intent, it is thought that the wall was a defensive barrier. One might expect that Singaporeans would be concerned about attack from the sea and that they might build a fortification to protect from that risk. However, due to its location, scholars speculate that the wall served as a defense from a land-based invasion and that the residents must have had sufficient confidence in their naval prowess to fend off a frontal sea-based assault. Further, the investment in a large, immovable structure in an area where traditionally groups relocated to contend with threats suggests early Singaporeans considered this position to be uncommonly promising as a port.

In addition, British colonists found evidence of structures built on what is now Fort Canning Hill, along with evidence of fruit orchards and terraces. Since ancient times in Southeast Asia, hills and mountains were associated with kingship and divinity. Thus, the hill that was only a little over a mile from the mouth of the Singapore River would be a logical place for the ruler to establish his residence, as suggested in the legends of the *Malay Annals*. The local lore when the British arrived in the early 1800s also supported the idea of a royal residence, with local people expressing unwillingness to go up on the hill, known to them as the Forbidden Hill, as it was the site of spirits. The Englishman credited with establishing Singapore as a British colony centuries later, Sir Thomas Stamford Raffles, wrote in a letter that if he died in Singapore and were buried on the hill, he would in death "have the honour of mixing with those of ashes of Malayan kings . . ."[1] During excavations for a reservoir in the 1920s, items of gold jewelry were found, including rings, earrings, an arm band, and what was likely a head ornament. Certainly these items would much more likely have been the possessions of a royal person than common people. Excavations by archeologists in recent decades have found the remains of various ceramics, porcelain, and other objects at three different locations around the Singapore River and Fort Canning Hill.

The Fort Canning Hill remains were of a higher quality than the others, offering further evidence that it was the residence of elites, as the old legends suggested.

The records strongly support the notion that Singapore was a political center in the 1300s, but its real power and fame was due to its role as a port. Fourteenth century Singapore seems to fit at least in part the definition of a port of trade in which trade is less a function of the economy and more a function of government policy; thus trading would have been highly structured and institutionalized, with government agents playing key roles in port activities. Reports from Portuguese traders, in particular, suggest that Singapore operated in such a manner. Traders' reports from various countries also indicate that Singapore was a point of exchange, rather than a source for goods. Local products were limited in type and were widely regarded to be of low quality. Chinese traders reported that there were few agricultural products due to poor soil. Local trade items were tin, hornbill casques (an ivory-like part of the hornbill bird, which was valued for carved ornaments), some wooden items, and cotton. Commonly traded products included a variety of fabrics (cottons and satins), iron rods, iron pots, and porcelains. The increase in activities by Chinese traders seems especially significant for Singapore and its trade. Various traders reported that, by this time, there was a permanent Chinese settlement in Singapore living peaceably with the indigenous population. This could have made the port especially comfortable and desirable for Chinese traders. Still, it is also clear from the reports of traders that pirate activities once again threatened ships. One of the best-known commentators of the time was Chinese merchant Wang Dayuan, who described the risks,

> When junks [Chinese boats] sail to the Western Ocean the local barbarians allow them to pass unmolested but when on their return the junks reach Ji-li-men [an island in the mouth of the Melaka Strait], the sailors prepare their armour and padded screens as a protection against arrows for, of a certainty, some two or three hundred pirate prahus [small boats] will put out to attack them for several days. Sometimes [the junks] are fortunate enough to escape with a favouring wind; otherwise the crews are butchered and the merchandise made off with in quick time.[2]

An early nineteenth century Malay author, Abdullah Munshi, indicated that the lore of Singaporean pirates was still strongly present at that time. He gave a grisly description of pirate activities, indicating that once a ship was taken, the pirates would bring it back to Singapore where they would kill the crew and either divide the spoils among themselves or fight each other to the death to gain the spoils. The description continues to describe the shores of what is now Sentosa Island as having "hundreds of human skulls rolling about on the sand; some old, some new, others with hair sticking to them, some with the teeth filed and others without."[3] While the lore may have been enhanced by passing time, the similarities to Wang's contemporaneous account corroborates Wang's account of the brutality and butchery that could befall traders in Singapore's waters where the locals were, in Wang's words, "addicted to piracy."[4]

While there were clear descriptions of the risks of trading in Singapore, it is nevertheless noteworthy the frequency with which traders of the time referred to Temasek in their writings. Wang's descriptions were of the area called the Dragon's Tooth Strait, thought by some scholars to refer to rock formations that, prior to their destruction, sat at the western entrance of what is today known as Keppel Harbour. Other scholars speculate that the Dragon's Tooth Strait was what is now known as the Singapore Main Strait, about 10 miles south of Singapore. Either way, evidence indicates that this area was in the immediate vicinity of Singapore and that fourteenth-century references to the Dragon's Tooth Strait referred to the port of Singapore. There was also a reference to Temasek in a memorial written in honor of a Vietnamese prince, who was said to be able to translate for Malay emissaries from Temasek. Further, a Javanese poem of the time also refers to Temasek. With such a variety of references to Temasek, ranging geographically from China to Vietnam to Java, it is clear that Singapore was known for its importance as a port well beyond vicinity of modern day Indonesia or Malaysia.

Scholars have found that Singapore's rise as a trade-post developed concurrently with other major developments in world trade of the time. While China may have been feeling pressured by the power of the Mongol Empire, elsewhere the power of the Mongols was having a broader positive effect. Called the Pax Mongolica or Mongolian Peace, the Mongol influence over both the overland and maritime Silk Roads provided a context in which a new global trading system could develop. Previously, shipping occurred on long-distance routes from the Far East to India or even further west to the Arabian Peninsula, which was relatively costly, risky, and time-consuming. However, the new trading system involved the division of the Maritime Silk Road into three segments: an Indian Ocean sector linking the Gulf of Aden and the Strait of Hormuz-based Arab traders to India, a Bay of Bengal sector linking the Indian ports with the Strait of Melaka and its associated ports (including Singapore), and a South China Sea sector linking Southeast Asia with southern China.

Much of this shift in trade patterns came about through the development of an Islamic-based institutional structure developed by Arab traders who began trading on the Maritime Silk Road as early as the seventh century. This institutional structure provided a system for raising capital, establishing credit, transporting and storing goods, resolving disputes, and providing information about supply and demand and other factors that would promote trade. The formalized structure assisted with the development of trust and confidence that obligations would be met by trading partners. This trust permitted the subdivision of the trade route, creating interdependence among traders. The gradual expansion of Islam that in part accompanied this trade also facilitated the adoption of this Islamic trading system. The Islamic, north-India-based Mughal Empire left its mark on the Indian Subcontinent and Islam spread to Southeast Asia as well, with majority Islamic populations still seen today in Malaysia and Indonesia. Singapore's growth as a significant port occurred at the time of this shift in global trading norms. Instead of one group of traders attempting to cover the entire Maritime Silk Road, more exchange happened with different trade groups covering different segments of the route. While the Islamic trading system seems to have been of fundamental global importance, it should be noted that the commonalities of Buddhism provided similar benefits of trust and confidence to other traders. The Srivijayan Empire was, in fact, a major Buddhist center and this seems to have assisted with Singapore's eventual ascent to prominence due to its founder coming from the Srivijayan center of Palembang.

This era of Singapore's history lasted through five rulers, according to the *Malay Annals*, or a period of about 100 years. However, while Singapore clearly prospered in its role as a port, this period of growth and rise to prominence was not untroubled. There were several larger, expansionist kingdoms in the region that prompted early Singaporeans to exercise awareness and caution. One of these, posing a threat from the north, was a Thai kingdom. The other, pressing from the south, was the Majapahit Empire based in Java. These concerns may have motivated Singaporeans to construct the previously mentioned fortification wall, indicating Singapore's promise and prominence. The precise relationship between Singapore and these two regional powers is unclear, but there are suggestions of Singapore having the status of vassal state to both the Majapahit Empire and the Thai kingdom.

The *Malay Annals* contain a legend of a Majapahit siege that was perhaps provoked by a Singaporean ruler not providing the proper respect and tributes that would have been due the overlord of a vassal state. At the time, Singapore's defenses included not only the fortified earthen wall but also a stockade-type structure made of wood. The Singaporeans withstood this initial Majapahit attack, but that did not remain the case.

There are a wider range of sources detailing accounts of a second Majapahit attack on Singapore, although the accounts vary somewhat. The *Malay Annals* indicate that Sri Sultan Iksander Shah, the fourth son of Sang Nila Utama and the fifth ruler of Singapore, had heard unpleasant rumors about his mistress, so he shamed her publicly. Her father, a treasury officer, was enraged by the public shaming and for revenge betrayed the ruler to the Majapahit by leaving open a gate to the fortified city. This enabled a subsequent Majapahit attack, with allegedly thousands of Majapahit landing on the beaches and storming the city once the gate was opened. While dates are uncertain, there are indications that this occurred in 1378. Some Singaporeans may have fled into the jungle, surviving the Majapahit attack and trying to rebuild afterward. However, these efforts, according to some accounts, came to nothing due to a threat from the Thai kingdom to the north. The Thais allegedly attacked and left the city a dependency until invading again in 1391, killing the ruler they had earlier put in place and completely destroying the city. Another account, written by the son of a Portuguese viceroy who led conquests in the region in the early 1500s, reported that the fifth ruler of Singapore was a usurper from Palembang named Parmeswara, who came to Singapore and shortly thereafter killed his host, the fourth ruler, and became the ruler for eight years. The brother of the assassinated leader was the ruler of Patani, part of an island southeast of the Philippines. He drove out Parmeswara with the support of the local people who never offered their trust or loyalty to the man who assumed power by murdering their leader. Another account by European colonists was very similar and written about the same time, but indicated that Parmeswara was driven out by the king of Siam (Thailand), who was the father-in-law of the murdered king of Singapore. Yet another account by colonial writers suggests that Singapore was under the authority of the Kingdom of Pahang on the Malay Peninsula, whose leader was a relative of the Singapore harbor master. Parmeswara killed the harbor master, provoking an assault on Singapore. Yet another colonial writer offered an account mirroring that of the *Malay Annals*. A final account indicates that Parmeswara was expelled from Palembang for some reason and then spent the next six years, from 1391 or 1392 to 1397 or 1398, ruling Singapore. While the details of the events cannot be known with certainty, it seems likely that Singapore was a vassal state of either the Majapahit or Thailand or perhaps both at different times. In addition to the more widely reported Majapahit attack on Singapore, the Chinese merchant Wang also reported an unsuccessful attack by Thai armies in the mid- to late 1340s. Further, while the accounts of that fifth ruler's ascension to the throne and the sources of conflict within his reign vary, there is a reasonable amount of consensus that at the end of his ruling period of six to eight years, Parmeswara was either forced out of Singapore or was compelled to flee.

KINGDOM OF MELAKA, 1398–1511

Parmeswara's departure marks a significant change in Singapore's fortunes and its future course. He did not flee and disappear into obscurity, though. Instead, he established a new kingdom slightly north of Singapore along the Melaka River (now western Malaysia) before he died in 1411. This Kingdom of Melaka became an important regional power and trade port, completely eclipsing Singapore and leaving Singapore to fade into relative obscurity, with only occasional mentions in the historical record after its decline.

While the Majapahit Empire seems to have conquered Singapore, its practice was not simply to take control of a territory and govern it as its own. Instead, the Majapahits raided a city, looted the wealth, enslaved the population, and burned any structures still standing. In this context, it is not surprising that Singapore did not exist as a port to rival Melaka once Parmeswara fled, as there was likely little remaining. The little that may have remained ultimately would have been under the authority of the Melakan ruler. A reference to Temasek in the writings of Chinese Admiral Zheng He notes his passage through the Dragon's Tooth Strait in the early 1420s. Archeologists have also found shards of pottery from various parts of Southeast Asia, specifically Thailand, Myanmar, and Vietnam, that date from the century after Parmeswara's flight. Such items indicate human activities near the mouth of the Singapore River but not on the royal ground of Fort Canning Hill, providing further evidence that Singapore was not completely abandoned after the elites left and that trade activities were ongoing, if less prominent. Similar evidence from later centuries is also present along the Kallang Estuary, not too far from the Singapore River. Thus, after the departure of Parmeswara, there was a serious decline in the political and economic stature of Singapore, but not a complete abandonment of this once-significant port.

The subsequent years saw an increase in piracy in the area, and it seems the leader of Melaka was able to establish the city as an important port because he offered protection from the pirates and a convenient location in the Strait of Melaka to provision ships. Chinese imperial records indicate that Parmeswara was a prominent leader. A Chinese delegation was sent to Melaka as early as 1401; and in 1405, Parmeswara returned to China with the delegation, was presented at court, and sought and received diplomatic recognition from China. He also offered Melaka as a base for China's fleets under Admiral Zheng He. This connection with China provided Melaka with certain benefits, including patronage from China and a measure of protection that would be associated with such patronage. Anyone seeking to interfere with Melaka's trade would know that he was also interfering with the interests of a much larger power, China. Parmeswara's successor, perhaps strategically, converted to Islam, which included Melaka in the Islamic trading system, making this a desirable port of call to still more traders. This connection to the Islamic traders who dominated the Maritime Silk Road was important to Melaka because it was this trading network that met European demand for Asian products. Wealth followed, as Melakan rulers insisted that ships call at the port. To better control shipping in the Strait, leading both to greater security for the shipping and increased wealth, the Melakan rulers expanded their territorial control from the eastern side of the Strait (the Malay Peninsula) to the western side of the Strait (the island of Sumatra) and increased their naval power by tapping into the traditional alliances like that with the *Orang Laut*. However, this new power center proved to be relatively short-lived due to external challenges of a fundamentally different nature that would also change the fate of Singapore and the region.

Rather than facing regional challenges, the European colonial powers made their presence felt in Southeast Asia, first the Portuguese, then the Dutch, and finally the English. In 1488, Portuguese seafarer Bartolomeu Diaz was the first European to encounter southern Africa's Cape of Good Hope. In 1497, fellow Portuguese explorer, Vasco de Gama built on Diaz's success and sailed around the Cape of Good Hope, demonstrating to Europeans that India and access to the trade riches that lay beyond it could be reached by circumnavigating Africa. This opened the door for a flood of European traders seeking the wealth via the Maritime Silk Road. In 1502, Portuguese Admiral Alfonso de Albuquerque set sail for India. He was appointed viceroy of the

Portuguese Indies and went on to capture the Indian city of Goa, making it the capital of Portugal's eastern interests. From Goa, he traveled further east for more conquest. By 1511, he had set his sights on Melaka because of its significance as a regional trading center. The Portuguese fleet was well-armed; the Melakans were not. The battle for Melaka reportedly lasted for days, but while the Melakans possessed a few fire arms, they mostly relied on bows and arrows, spears, and other primitive weapons, whereas the Portuguese had heavy arms and armor. The Portuguese took control of the Strait and the port city and built a stone fortress to protect their interests. Like the Melakan rulers, they charged duties for passing through the Strait, which they controlled for the next 100 years.

KINGDOM OF JOHOR, 1511–1699

The defeated Melakan sultan, Mahmud, decided to reestablish a settlement in a different location and selected a place on the Johor River, which flows in to the Johor Strait, the small body of water separating Singapore from peninsular Malaysia. He then moved his capital to the island of Bintan, just to the southeast of Singapore and the Malay Peninsula in what is today Indonesia, but this settlement was attacked repeatedly by the Portuguese and ultimately destroyed in 1526. However, Bintan was significant because it provided a connection to the historical source of noble authority from Queen Sakidar Shah and the founding of Singapore by Sang Nila Utama. Since the Portuguese made a successful settlement at Bintan impossible, Sultan Mahmud relocated again, to Kampar on the island of Sumatra, where he died two years later. His successor, Ala-ud-din, attempted to establish his administrative capital on the Johor River and built a protective fort a few miles downstream. The following decades saw repeated battles with the Portuguese, which the Johor forces repulsed with some success, although Ala-ud-din eventually made a peace agreement with the Portuguese. Despite the defeat to the Portuguese and the repeated relocations of the capital shortly thereafter, Johor became an important actor in the region.

The primary power shifted from Melaka to Johor, but Singapore still merited mention in the writings of maritime traders of the time. Johor is in the immediate vicinity of Singapore but far enough away to offer different port opportunities. There are reports that, following the defeat of Melaka by the Portuguese, a Melakan admiral established operations in Singapore. Tomé Pires, a Portuguese trader and author of *Suma Oriental*, a primary source about the maritime trade routes of the time, reported in 1515 that the inhabitants of the Singapore channel area lived in a few unimportant villages. He referred to Singapore as a "kingdom," but one with very little territory. Pires also noted that Chinese merchants still called at Singapore, a fact supported by archeological findings of sixteenth century Chinese porcelain fragments around the Kallang Estuary, reflecting activity in Singapore in a different location from the earlier trading venue. Another Portuguese writer, Joe de Lisboa, reported in 1526 that a town in Singapore had been destroyed by the Portuguese. Reports from the late 1500s continue to mention Singapore, as well, and both Portuguese and Dutch documents from the early 1600s mention the presence of a harbor master, which is a person of great significance in the Malay royal establishment. The harbor master would not only collect taxes from foreign merchant ships entering the harbor but also control most other aspects of harbor life, such as transporting and warehousing goods and deciding where foreign merchants could live. The fact that Singapore had a harbor master at this time indicates that it was still an active port for international shipping. Thus, as global shipping and trade entered a different phase with the emergence of important European powers in the region, Singapore continued to be tied to the trade networks that comprised the globalization of that age.

Regional conflict came to the fore again, as relative shifts in power among groups led to strained relations. Officials from Portugal and Johor had established a working relationship but toward the middle of the 1500s, Aceh, a Sumatra-based kingdom, was an ascendant and expansionist power. Given its location at the northern end of the Strait of Melaka, tensions with the Portuguese over control of shipping increased, as did tensions with Johor over rival claims to be the legitimate successors to the Srivijayan Empire. The tensions culminated in a naval battle between the Portuguese and Acehnese in 1577 just off the coast of Changi, Singapore. The Johor-Portuguese cooperation broke down in the 1580s over trade-related disagreements, and Johor besieged Portuguese-controlled Melaka in 1586–1587. In the context of these strained relations, Johor was attacked in the mid- to late sixteenth century and into the seventeenth century by both the Portuguese and the Acehnese, including the burning of Singapore in 1613 by the Portuguese, since Singapore was connected to Johor through its Melakan heritage and Singaporean heritage before Melaka. As an indicator of shifting alliances, Johor and Aceh teamed up in 1616 to attack Portuguese-controlled Melaka, but to no avail. The Johor sultans, being flexible, were often willing to simply move to a different location along the Johor River and continue their trading operations, thus maintaining an advantage over Aceh, allowing Johor to thrive despite greater rivalries.

Around this same time, in the early 1600s, the region experienced yet another significant shift in power as the Dutch became active in challenging the Portuguese monopoly on trade to Europe along the Maritime Silk Road. The primary rivalry between the Portuguese and the Dutch sometimes played out in direct conflicts, such as in 1603 when they fought a battle in the Singapore Strait or as in 1611 when the Portuguese complained that the Dutch were building a fort in the Singapore Strait area. However, given the importance of indigenous regional power centers, such as Johor and Aceh, the Portuguese-Dutch rivalry spilled over and touched these regional powers, alliances, and rivalries. The Dutch entered the area in the context of the Dutch East India Company, which was a joint-stock company, a professionally-managed corporation with shareholders who were part owners and could buy and sell their stocks. The company was incorporated in 1602 and was unique in the powers it had been granted by the Dutch government. It could negotiate on behalf of the state, and enter into contracts, treaties, and alliances; it could take over territories, build forts in the territories it controlled, appoint governors for those territories, raise an army, and even mint its own coins. It is likened to a state within a state, since it was the Dutch government granting such extensive authority. Between selling shares of the company and the ability to issue short- and long-term bonds to raise capital, the Dutch East India Company (DEIC) had substantial wealth. This wealth, coupled with aggressiveness, led it to amass enormous economic and political power. From 1602 to 1696, the dividends it paid its shareholders ranged from a low of 12 percent to a high of 63 percent.[5] Its charter was renewed by the government every 20 years in exchange for financial compensation. The DEIC propelled the Netherlands to a position as a leading global trading power in the seventeenth century.

Initially, the Dutch were a useful ally for Johor. In 1603, they launched a joint assault on a Portuguese merchant ship off the coast of Singapore. The Portuguese continued to launch assaults on Johor's ever-moving capital and also blockaded the Johor River. Johor's trade was harmed badly, and they turned to the Dutch for assistance. The Dutch fought a naval battle with the Portuguese that ended the blockade and formed the foundation for a closer alliance between Johor and the DEIC.

However, while the Dutch may not have been concerned about challenging the trading power of Johor, they were very concerned about the power of the Portuguese. In a letter to the directors of the United Amsterdam Company, a branch of the DEIC, company representative Jacob van Heemskerck described interactions with the king of Johor and the assault on the Portuguese merchant ship. He also discussed how important and profitable the trade with China was to the Portuguese. He urged the company to send good ships so that they could attempt to break the Portuguese monopoly and enter into this lucrative Chinese trade themselves. The letter strategically analyzed different options for setting up a trade center, and Johor was near the top of the list behind Melaka. Heemskerck considered Melaka to be more desirable because of its defenses. The Portuguese elite were already living in stone houses and there was a stone wall protecting the town. These fortifications would allow the Dutch to better protect the wealth of the DEIC from hazards like fire or enemy assault. If they could not gain control of Melaka, then Johor was the next best choice, weaker in fortification but equal in strategic location. Heemskerck further argued that if the Company could gain control of textile trade at Johor, then Melaka could be effectively besieged. Moreover, the Portuguese would not dare sail to China with the DEIC's ships at the mouth of the Johor River, and the DEIC would be able to take control of trade with China and Japan. These lofty ambitions to assert Dutch strength and to transform the existing trading patterns highlights the prominence that the Singapore region had in the global trade network of the time—the region was a linchpin of power in global trade.

Subsequent developments for the Dutch cast fortune on Johor, although it may not initially have been apparent. In 1612, the Dutch captured control of Jakarta, then known as Batavia, on the north end of the island of Java, with access to the Strait of Sunda that runs between the islands of Sumatra and Java. While farther from Indian trade routes than the Strait of Melaka, the Strait of Sunda offered a slightly shorter route to the Cape of Good Hope and around the southern part of Africa, thus being a preferable route for trade directly from Indonesia, in particular the trade of spices from the Moluccas (formerly the Spice Islands) to Europe or the Spice Route. The DEIC established its headquarters there, and it became the center for what would become the Dutch trading empire in Southeast Asia. This lessened the importance of the Strait of Melaka for Dutch trading and kept their attention focused well to the southwest of the Johor-Singapore-Melaka area.

While the territory around the Strait of Melaka was no longer of critical import, weakening the Portuguese hold on trade in East and Southeast Asia remained a top priority for the Dutch. The less trade that was controlled by Portugal, the greater the wealth that could be amassed by the DEIC. In 1640–1641, Johor joined the Dutch in besieging Melaka, and this time they succeeded. The Portuguese were driven from Southeast Asia. At about the same time, Acehnese power was also in decline following the death of their leader. The Portuguese and Acehnese were out of the way; and while the Dutch still controlled Melaka, they primarily focused on their regional headquarters at Jakarta (formerly Batavia), 500 miles to the south. This left an opening for Johor to exert its power in the area around Singapore.

Despite peaceful coexistence with the new European power, regional rivalries would rise again. Jambi, another Malay kingdom based on the island of Sumatra, challenged Johor's power and status as a trading center and sacked the Johor capital in 1673. Johor regrouped, revenged itself on Jambi, and reasserted its strength as a meaningful port in the international trading system. The Dutch, still preoccupied to the south, paid little attention and observed from afar.

KINGDOM OF JOHOR-RIAU AND THE BUGIS YEARS, 1699–1818

Johor's reemergence following the Jambi attack was short-lived. This time, the problems that arose were internal, and they brought the ancient Palembang-Singapore-Melaka-Johor ruling line to an end. People in territories controlled by Johor were unhappy with the domineering role played by Johor and its ruling sultan, Mahmud. Both local and European reports from the time mentioned various sadistic acts that Mahmud committed against the people of Johor. In 1699, Mahmud was assassinated by his own ruling council, which not only upset the line of succession since the sultan had no direct heir but also rattled traditional loyalties that had provided some stability to the Johor sultanate.

The *Orang Laut*, who had been loyal to the royal line throughout all of its changes of leader and location, were an important part of the power structure of Johor and had at times across the centuries proved a key force in the defenses of the sultanate. The ties had been based heavily on personal loyalty to the sultan. There was a strong patronage-based relationship in which the *Orang Laut*, in exchange for loyalty, strength, stability, and esteem, were rewarded with wealth and inclusion. The new line of leaders came from non-royal chief ministers, the first being Abdul Jalil. The *Orang Laut* transferred some of their loyalties to the new leadership but never to the same degree as they had to the royal line with its semi-divine origins. This compromised the established power structure and undermined long-term stability.

The next major change that came about after the death of the sultan was the rise of a new regional power. The Bugis people arrived as immigrants from Sulawesi (formerly Celebes), an island east of Borneo in today's Indonesia. The Bugis were mercenaries who worked for various sultans on the Malay Peninsula. However, with time, they gained considerable power and became highly influential in the leadership of various kingdoms, including Johor. The rise of the Bugis was so significant that the 1700s are considered the century of the Bugis in Malay history. For the internally weakened Johor government, the increasing influence of the Bugis further disrupted previous power structures and undermined stability.

Another power shift occurred when, in 1717, Raja Kecik from Siak, a Sumatran area of the Melaka-Johor sultanate's holdings, arrived and bluffed his way onto the throne. The people, seemingly thinking he could be a countervailing force to the rising power of the Bugis, played along. He was backed by a Sumatran ruler and arrived in the Johor capital, then in the Riau Islands, southeast of Singapore, in 1718 with a large Sumatran military force. The *Orang Laut* sided with this new leader, too, and for a time he was able to take power. Before long, though, the Bugis asserted their power and removed him from the throne. The Bugis then became the de facto rulers of Johor, adopting the title of "junior king" for their leader of Johor, relative to the name for the Malay leader, "great king." With this the Johor sultanate took on a hybridized Malay-Bugis identity, leading to complexities that ultimately made the leadership vulnerable to the manipulations of European colonial powers.

After being dethroned, Kecik returned to Siak and established a Malay sultanate and set out to challenge Bugis domination of shipping in the Melaka-Singapore-Riau area with raids on shipping and occasionally full battles. The conflict also broadened to involve the Dutch, who were still formally in control of Melaka, despite their greater degree of activity based around Jakarta and the Strait of Sunda. There was also a significant degree of internal conflict facing Johor, again increasing instability in the sultanate. Sultan Suleiman, a puppet of the Bugis, desired more independence and, in 1755, made an agreement with the Dutch to help him gain greater autonomy and control over territory. The Bugis retaliated by attacking Dutch Melaka, a failed effort; then the Dutch retaliated by attacking the Bugis at the island of Lingga, south of the Riau Islands and Singapore. The Bugis-Dutch conflict went on for several years until the Bugis were defeated and a peace agreement was signed in 1758. This also resulted in an agreement to give Dutch exclusive tin rights, something Suleiman had initially granted the Dutch in return for their assistance. The following year there was a Bugis coup, placing Daeng Kamboja in power. However, instability continued after Sultan Suleiman died in 1760. The Bugis killed the sultan's successor and took back control of the Johor Sultanate. The Bugis-Siak rivalry rose to the fore again when Raja Ismail of Siak fought a naval battle with Bugis forces from Johor-Riau led by Daeng Kamboja. This well-documented battle took place on the Singapore River in 1767. Archeological evidence, specifically coins of the Dutch East India Company dating 1730–1796, has been found near the mouth of the Singapore and indicates that Singapore continued to be an active port through this time.

The tumultuous relations continued between the three power rivals (Johor, Siak, and the Dutch) for some years, and instability within Bugis Johor was likewise ongoing. The peace agreement between Johor and the Bugis collapsed in 1782 when the Bugis began raiding Dutch possessions in the Strait of Melaka. The Dutch retaliated by destroying the raiding Bugis ships and then driving the Bugis out of Riau, the governing headquarters of Johor. The Dutch demanded the Bugis leadership acknowledge formally via a treaty that Johor-Riau was a Dutch port and the kingdom a Dutch holding. The Dutch also demanded agreement for a Dutch governor and garrison to be stationed at Riau. Thus, for the first time, there was formal European control of the successor sultanate to the Singapore-Melaka-Johor line. The Bugis tried again in 1785, one year after the treaty was signed, to win back Johor, but they failed. Bugis Sultan Mahmud's next attempt to broaden the conflict was in 1787. He sought regional support by appealing for help to Sultan Illanun of Borneo to oust the Dutch. The Bornean forces succeeded in capturing Riau but held it for themselves until the Dutch quickly regained control, while Sultan Mahmud fled.

The various changes of authority created a much less stable sultanate than had previously existed when Singapore, Melaka, and Johor were able to fend off challenges, sometimes through strategic relocations, but they remained active and relatively prosperous powers in the ever-changing global system of trade. The internal divisions, challenges for authority, and competing claims of legitimate rule that troubled the sultanate under Bugis control set a foundation for the full colonization of the area with the arrival of yet another influential European actor: the English East India Company.

The English East India Company (EEIC) was also a joint-stock company, modeled on the Dutch East India Company. Queen Elizabeth I granted the charter on December 31, 1600, giving the company exclusive trading rights in the Indies as long as it did not challenge the established trading rights of "any Christian prince." King James I granted the company a perpetual charter a few years later in 1609. Through the eighteenth century, the English were most interested in trade with India and concentrated their efforts most fully there, although certainly not exclusively. EEIC Captain Hamilton provided an account of his meeting in 1703 with Johor Sultan Abdul Jalil while en route to China. He reported,

> [The sultan] treated me very kindly, and made me a present of the Island of Singapura, but I told him it could be of no use to a private person tho' [*sic*] a proper Place for a Company to settle a Colony on, lying in the Center of Trade, and being accommodated with good Rivers and safe Harbours, so conveniently situated, that all the Winds served Shipping both go out and come into these rivers.[6]

Hamilton also visited the island and gave it close inspection, as he gave descriptions of its soil, timber, and sugar cane. While no one knows for certain why the Johor leader would have offered the English such real estate (perhaps seeking an ally in the tumultuous situation that was developing with the Bugis and Dutch), it is certainly noteworthy that the English had the opportunity to gain the island much earlier than the establishment of their colony of Singapore and turned it down.

The EEIC's initial forays into Southeast Asia took place after the founding of the company, but its successes were extremely limited. It sought to gain trade in the region and on the Malay Peninsula in particular, but the Dutch were successful in combating the competition and closing down the British trading ports in Southeast Asia. The one exception was Bengkulu (formerly Bencoolen) on the southwest coast of Sumatra, although it was not considered an ideal location. The difficulties of establishing thriving trade in Southeast Asia led the EEIC to concentrate its efforts on India. However, the English were not by any means disinterested in trade with China, and as historical trade patterns have shown, easy access to ports in Southeast Asia greatly facilitated that trade. The importing of Chinese tea, for example, transformed English society, giving rise to the idea of teahouses and time spent talking over cups of tea. This practice became an institution; and to meet the rising demand of this fashionable activity, large amounts of tea had to be imported from China. This led to a serious imbalance of trade for England that needed remedy. In addition to helping introduce opium to China and establishing a monopoly for the Chinese opium trade, the English also took careful note of what products from Southeast Asia the Chinese regularly imported. These included edible birds nest, hornbill casques, pepper, tin, tortoise shell, beeswax, and other products. Despite the past focus on Indian trade, some in the EEIC came to see the greater desirability of controlling ports in Southeast Asia, and in 1786, the English successfully established a port operation to service their India-China trade at Penang on the Malay Peninsula.

Underscoring the international nature of the forces affecting Southeast Asia, it was political conflict in Europe that helped shift power toward the English in Southeast Asia. In Europe, Napoleon had taken control of France and was waging war to expand the French Empire. The Napoleonic Wars, a series of conflicts between France and an alliance of opponents, took place from 1792 to 1815 when Napoleon was defeated at the Battle of Waterloo. In the context of these conflicts, in 1795, Napoleon invaded and occupied the Netherlands and eventually made it a part of the French Empire. The English, concerned about the rising power of France and a part of the allied opposition to counter it, were worried about the possible implications of French control of the Netherlands on their Asian trade. The English government ordered the English East India Company to take over temporarily some of the holdings of the Dutch East India Company, with the holdings to be returned at the end of the conflict; Melaka was taken over in 1795 and Jakarta in 1803. However, once it came time to return control, the Dutch East India Company had ceased to exist and it was the representatives of the Dutch government who returned for their holdings.

Having had control of the region, it was distasteful to some in the English East India Company to lose ground again to the Dutch. They saw it as perilous for their trade with China, particularly if the Dutch reasserted their authority in the Strait of Melaka to the Riau Archipelago area south of Singapore. However, the Governor-General of the EEIC, Francis Rawdon-Hastings, Earl of Moria and Marquess of Hastings (Lord Hastings), was forbidden from acting because the English Crown feared war with the Dutch. With time, however, trade priorities changed the opinions of important people.

Singapore's early history is a function of its geographic location and advantageous port features that made it a recurrent focal point for world trade. From the beginning of trade, when boats sailed the entire distance from China to the Middle East or India while needing ports of call for provisions, to the eventual segmentation of the Maritime Silk

Road, where different traders would specialize in different segments of the road, needing ports to trade goods, to finally the arrival of the European colonial trading empires, Singapore's location at the mouth of the Strait of Melaka made it desirable real estate. While its fortunes rose and fell and while it may have fallen into relative obscurity as a port, compared to Melaka, Johor, or Bintan Island, some trade activities continued, proving that Singapore was in its ancient history a notable port of call in the globalized trading and shipping networks of the time.

NOTES

1. Quoted in Cheryl-Ann Low Mei Gek, "Singapore from the 14th–19th Century," in Early *Singapore 1300s-1879: Evidences in Maps, Texts and Artifacts*, ed. John N. Miksic and Cheryl-Ann Low Mei Gek (Singapore: Singapore History Museum, 2004), 14–40.

2. Quoted in Malcolm Murfett et al., *Between Two Oceans* (New York, NY: Marshall Cavendish International, 2004), 25.

3. Ibid., 26.

4. Quoted in John N. Miksic, "14th Century Singapore: A Port of Trade," in Early *Singapore 1300s–1879: Evidences in Maps, Texts and Artifacts*, ed. John N. Miksic and Cheryl-Ann Low Mei Gek (Singapore: Singapore History Museum, 2004), 41–54.

5. Jaap Harskamp, "A Colonial Obsession: Dutch Narrative Literature on the East Indies 1800–1945" (catalogue of holdings in the British Library, http://www.bl.uk/reshelp/pdfs/dutbibcolonial.pdf), 4.

6. Quoted in Malcolm Murfett et al., *Between Two Oceans* (New York, NY: Marshall Cavendish International, 2004), 36.

3

The Establishment of Colonial Singapore: 1819–1867

The founding of Singapore as a colony of the English East India Company (EEIC), based in Kolkata (formerly Calcutta), India, was an outcome of the global political and economic competitions of its time. With Napoleon having been defeated in Europe and the Netherlands once again independent, the Dutch were resurgent in Southeast Asia and once again a threat to Britain's trade with China. This trade was crucial to Britain because it was seen as the country's path to ever greater prosperity.

THE CONTEXT FOR COLONIZATION

For many years, the sole British holding in the region was Bengkulu (formerly Bencoolen) on the island of Sumatra. Initially established because it was far enough away from the Dutch trading center of Jakarta (formerly Batavia) but close to lucrative pepper-growing areas of Sumatra, the Bengkulu settlement proved over its 140 years to be a disappointment. Too far from main trading routes and largely a financial drain, it was considered a remote venue where ineffective EEIC staffers could cause little harm. Still, the British were loath to abandon the outpost because it was a toehold in a valuable region dominated by the Dutch. In 1818 Sir Thomas Stamford Raffles, the person primarily associated with the founding of Singapore, was posted there. Previously, Raffles had been posted to Penang on the Malay Peninsula, where the British established themselves in 1786. In Penang, Raffles learned the Malay language and history, and he maintained a correspondence with Malay nobles. This prior experience, combined with what he found in Bengkulu in terms of the expanding influence in the area of the Dutch, were chief motivations for Raffles in advocating for the establishment of an EEIC colony in Singapore. Given how the colony developed, however, it is also worth noting that Raffles was an idealist and a visionary, and his idea for the new colony was to create a place where liberal, Enlightenment ideas could be applied (ending slavery, providing education, etc.). While commercial interests were foremost in creating a new colony, these idealistic notions were further impetus for his efforts.

Initially, Raffles sought to work from Penang to establish a secure trade route for EEIC trade with China. He believed if peace could be made with Aceh, which was across the Strait of Melaka from Penang, then that could serve as the company's route. He soon realized, however, that Penang was too far north of the critical narrow part of the Strait and that an EEIC holding in the area of the narrows would be required to secure reliable trade free of Dutch interference. While he had never visited Singapore in any of his previous travels in the region, Raffles had a familiarity with the early history of Singapore and was aware of the *Malay Annals* that identified Singapore as the original location of the still active Johor-Riau Sultanate. His interest in this historical legacy may also have heightened his interest in Singapore as the location for a future colony. The historical record is mixed, with some documents lacking any references to Singapore but others suggesting Singapore was in Raffles's sights all along.

In addition to international political and economic considerations, the political turmoil of the indigenous peoples also facilitated the colonization of Singapore. A succession dispute threw the Sultanate of Johor-Riau into disarray. Problems were bubbling already at the turn of the nineteenth century when the *temenggong*, a traditional, very high-ranking position of Malay nobility, roughly comparable to a minister of justice or defense, left the Riau area where the sultan was based. *Temenggong* Abdul Rahman had his traditional authority undermined by the strong influence of the Bugis in the court. *Temenggong*

Abdul Rahman set up his own operations in Singapore, just far enough away from the sultan's power center where he could have a fairly high degree of autonomy within a small area of influence. This development occurred in the first decade of the 1800s. In 1812 the puppet-sultan of the Bugis, Sultan Mahmud of Johor-Riau died, leaving behind no heirs born of royal mothers. His two sons, the elder Hussein, also known as Tengku Long and the younger, Abdul Rahman (the same name as the *Temenggong* but not the same person) were both born of commoner mothers. There are indications that succession was intended for the elder. For example, prominent marriages had been arranged with daughters of the *Temenggong* and another high ranking official in Malay courts, the *bendahara*, a title comparable to prime minister and commander in chief. However, the powerful Bugis supported the succession of the younger son. This was a logical choice for the Bugis; the marriage arrangements of the older son would create family ties between him and the formal titleholders of the Malay nobility who were the chief rivals of the Bugis for influence. The Bugis support was sufficient to leave Abdul Rahman the de facto successor; however, no official coronation could occur because the late sultan's royal wife supported the succession of the elder son, Hussein. She would not turn over the royal regalia (e.g., musical instruments supposedly dating back about five centuries to Queen Sakidar Shah) that were necessary for a legitimate coronation and rule. Thus, the situation remained unsettled until Hussein removed himself from the court environment and went to a remote location in the Riau islands, leaving Abdul Rahman to act as sultan.

THE ESTABLISHMENT OF THE COLONY

In order for Raffles to realize his vision for establishing a new colony, he had to gain the approval of the EEIC. He pitched his idea to the Governor-General of India, Lord Hastings, who approved limited authority to secure British trade through Melaka. Raffles went to Penang and enlisted the assistance of his long-time associate Colonel William Farquhar, sending Farquhar south with a small fleet of ships to investigate options. Raffles joined him a short time later, and after ruling out other locations such as Karimun Island in the middle of the Strait, Raffles and Farquhar weighed anchor off the coast of Singapore. The next day, on January 30, 1819 they landed near the mouth of the Singapore River and met with the *Temenggong*, quickly signing an agreement with him permitting the British to establish a trade settlement on the Singapore River. Documents show that early international traders had knowledge of Singapore's natural deep-water harbor, today known as Keppel Harbour, which is what eventually made Singapore such an outstanding site. However, Raffles seemed to have no idea of the excellence of Singapore's port offerings. Previous trade activity took place on the River and the Kallang Estuary, and evidence suggests that this is what Raffles imagined Singapore had to offer as a port. It seems that after Singapore fell into relative obscurity after the sultanate moved to Melaka, then Johor and Riau, the awareness of the deep-water harbor was lost to the international trading community.

Prior to his work with Raffles, Farquhar had been the Resident (chief administrator) of Melaka for more than a decade while the British held it for the Dutch during the Napoleonic Wars. This gave Farquhar, like Raffles, an intimate understanding of Malay culture and language. He had, in fact, married a Malay woman. His local insights meant that he was also familiar with the power struggle and succession crisis that was going on within the Sultanate of Johor-Riau. It is likely that the *Temenggong* also considered the strategic advantage that cooperation with the British could have in settling that matter in his favor. Since Abdul Rahman was de facto sultan, Farquhar was sent to ask his approval for the establishment of a trading settlement in Singapore. This was a rather sensitive effort, since Farquhar, as Resident of Melaka, had signed a treaty with Abdul Rahman providing for the security of British shipping and in signing the treaty effectively acknowledged Abdul Rahman as the new sultan. The Dutch, who held considerable influence with Abdul Rahman, were reasserting their authority in the Riau Archipelago and insisted the treaty be annulled. When Farquhar reached Bintan, where the court was based, Abdul Rahman denied him permission for the settlement. However, in the interim the *Temenggong* summoned the rival successor for the sultanate, Hussein, to Singapore. On February 6, 1819, Raffles signed an agreement with Hussein and the *Temenggong* in which the EEIC affirmed Hussein as Sultan and granted him $5,000 per year and the *Temenggong* $3,000 per year in exchange for the right to establish a trading settlement at Singapore.

The Dutch were angry when they heard of the British actions. The head of Dutch operations at Melaka recommended attacking the British and removing them from Singapore, an act that could have been accomplished with ease, given the tiny British force in Singapore and the enormous strength of Dutch troops and watercraft in the region. To make matters even more uncertain, Sultan Hussein and the *Temenggong* both wrote letters to Abdul Rahman and other officials, in an effort to cover their own perceived misdeeds, claiming that they had been coerced by the British into signing the treaty.

What likely staved off Dutch military action and allowed the British to establish a hold on Singapore were the mixed messages given by EEIC and British government officials to the Dutch. While Raffles and some in the EEIC were deeply concerned about keeping the Dutch away from Britain's China trade, others were instead contemplating turning away from Southeast Asia and granting it to the Dutch in exchange for Dutch holdings in India. The EEIC governor of Penang, who had not supported Raffles's mission to establish a more southern colony in the area, suggested to the Dutch that the EEIC would not agree to Raffles's arrangements with Hussein and the *Temenggong*. Moreover, the EEIC office in London had sent word to Kolkata forbidding the mission, although the word arrived too late; and the British Foreign Office told the Dutch government that Raffles had authority to establish commercial arrangements but not political ones. This led the Dutch to be more moderate in their response to the treaty, but the EEIC headquarters in Kolkata embraced the treaty and ordered more defensive forces sent to Singapore. The Foreign Office had been alarmed at what it would have to do to save face if the Dutch forcibly removed the British from Singapore, but when the Dutch failed to do so, the Foreign Office, too, supported the treaty. Thus, the little colony was established and largely unchallenged by the Dutch forces that could so easily have reversed Raffles's work.

Surviving the initial political uncertainties did not, however, guarantee Singapore an easy path. Raffles left Singapore almost immediately after signing the treaty, appointing Farquhar as Resident and leaving a series of instructions for how the colony should be established, specifically defensive arrangements and the policy designating Singapore a free port with no tariffs for trade. The first few months were difficult, with too little food to feed the additional mouths of the British. The local population numbered probably in the upper hundreds, with Malays making up the largest number of households, followed by various Orang peoples, and a small group of resident Chinese.[1] They had a subsistence existence gathering fruit and catching fish; the increase in numbers of people to feed was initially problematic. Combining that with the security threats from the Dutch and from local pirates, the new administration had numerous challenges. Farquhar, utilizing his ongoing connections in Melaka (despite it being in Dutch hands), sent for food and traders, and the Melakans responded. By April there was adequate food, and trade was beginning with settlers coming from Melaka. Raffles returned in June of 1819 and made more logistical arrangements, including another treaty with the Sultan that defined the territory of the British trading settlement, bordered on the west by Tanjong Malong, on the east by Tanjong Katon, and extending as far inland as a cannon shot. He also began city planning in Singapore, designating specific residential areas for the different ethnic communities and appointing people of each community to have oversight, maintain order, and settle disputes within their community. The *Temmengong* and Sultan had that responsibility for their respective followers, while Resident Farquhar had final decision-making authority in cases of appeal.

THE EARLY YEARS

With basic orders and provisions in place, Raffles returned to his governorship in Bengkulu. Farquhar was to report to him, but communications were poor at best, with Raffles often not replying to Farquhar's queries. Thus, aside from Raffles's basic policies, Farquhar was largely left alone to shape the development of the new colony. The most critical provision, Raffles's insistence on free trade at the port, had both its positives and negatives. Trade and immigration grew. Fed in part by Farquhar's reputation in Melaka, settlers flowed in to the burgeoning settlement. Immigration was further fed by Chinese who had settled in Southeast Asia to pursue private trade. They tended to move wherever trade conditions were favorable, and Singapore offered that through the lack of tariffs and the application of consistent laws and policies. A large group of disaffected Bugis, concerned about Dutch control of Riau, also moved to Singapore, which helped Singapore capture a significant portion of the substantial Bugis trade. However, on the negative side, the lack of tariffs also created severe financial restraints for the colony's administration. Raffles insisted on extremely lean budgets because he feared that the EEIC would not support the development of Singapore if it were a financial drain. Lacking financing from the company and prohibited from raising funds by charging for trade, Farquhar was left to find creative solutions. His efforts at cost restraints were so successful that administrative salaries for Singapore for a year were less costly than Bengkulu for a month.[2] To pay the bills, Farquhar implemented small port fees. He also disregarded Raffles's idealistic social mandates relating to moral behavior and raised additional funds by auctioning monopoly rights to the sale of opium, liquor, and gambling operations. Some of the funds were used for public works, which lent a sense of security to Singapore's future. Farquhar also arranged for the development of a local police force, funded in part by contributions from

European and Asian merchants, to address the developing problem of lawless behavior.

Raffles returned to Singapore in the fall of 1822 as a last stop before retirement due to poor health. Finding a thriving colony on his return, he reportedly felt reinvigorated and became active in the administration of Singapore. While he was pleased by Singapore's growth in population and thriving trade, he was extremely displeased by many of the choices Farquhar had made about policies for the colony and his revenue-seeking tactics. Raffles's idealism shone through clearly during this time, proving he was a visionary, although not necessarily a practical administrator. Within a few months, Raffles denounced Farquhar to Kolkata as incompetent, further humiliated him by reassigning some of his duties to more junior staffers, and finally, in spring of 1823, removed Farquhar as resident to take on the job himself and then stripped Farquhar of his military leadership role. Kolkata later restored Farquhar's good name and chastised Raffles for his poor treatment of Farquhar but not before Farquhar left Singapore, albeit with a warm send-off from the local merchants.

With the practical Farquhar out of the way, Raffles pursued his vision for the colony. Public works soon followed, including leveling a hill and filling in the southwest side of the Singapore River, which was too swampy to be useful. This reclaimed area, today known as Boat Quay, soon became the commercial center for the town. Raffles also relocated the *Temenggong*'s settlement away from the River, which freed the waterway for trade and also distanced the *Temenggong*'s followers, some of whom were problematically unruly, from the commercial center. Raffles also divvied up land to other groups. The Chinese were expected to comprise the bulk of future residents, so a significant area west of the River near the commercial center was set aside for them, with additional subdivisions for the different Chinese dialect groups.

Other major governance changes introduced by Raffles included easing the Sultan and *Temenggong* out of public life. In accordance with Malay tradition, Farquhar had let them have considerable influence within their communities and in the colony's affairs. Raffles, however, saw their involvement as an impediment to his goals for the colony and made efforts to marginalize them, even buying out their judicial authority over their followers and any land rights beyond their designated areas. Raffles also strongly reaffirmed Singapore's free trade status. He determined that the judicial system would be based on English law, except for situations relating to marriage, inheritance, and religious practice. In these practices, Malay laws could apply unless they were "contrary to reason, justice, or humanity."[3] A small measure of representative government was introduced by granting Europeans not affiliated with the EEIC a role in governance and legislation.

Issues of morality and social well-being also caught Raffles's attention. He focused on the prevention of crime and the rehabilitation (rather than punishment) of convicts. He banned carrying weapons hoping to decrease violence. He also banned what he considered to be the worst of the social ills: gambling and cockfighting. He levied heavy taxes to discourage the use of opium and alcohol and forbade men from living from the earnings of prostitutes. Raffles also banned slave trading in Singapore, which was mostly carried out by the Bugis, and declared that no one who had come to Singapore since the British first arrived could be considered a slave. He also limited indentured servitude. Finally, shortly before his final departure from Singapore in 1823, he used some of his personal funds to open a school for the non-European population, the Singapore Institution.

Upon Raffles's retirement, Singapore's status in the EEIC shifted, coming under direct control of Kolkata, rather than being overseen from Bengkulu. Raffles departure from Singapore and the company also led to the appointment of Singapore's third administrator, Resident Dr. John Crawfurd. Like Farquhar, Crawfurd was a pragmatist. He dismissed many of Raffles's goals and policies as unreasonably idealistic and reversed them. Raffles's plans for education, representative government, the justice system, and his moral standards fell by the wayside. Believing that gambling and cockfighting could not be eradicated, Crawfurd decided the government should profit by them and set up licensing agreements. He also earned revenue from opium and alcohol operations by setting up "revenue farms," strictly regulated, government-sanctioned monopolies that were sold by auction. After winning the auctions, the owners of the revenue farms also had to pay regular rent to the government, providing ongoing funding. Opium for export was freely traded, but that destined for the domestic market was too lucrative to be left unregulated. In fact, the colony's income from local opium operations usually constituted between 40 and 60 percent of locally collected revenue.[4] This was a significant departure from Raffles's vision. Gambling was eventually outlawed in 1829 and remained illegal on moral grounds despite recurrent discussions of restoring it for revenue purposes; however the opium dens remained open, thriving, and lucrative.

In contrast to his views of Raffles's idealism, Crawfurd strongly supported his predecessor's ideas relating to free trade and city planning, and he also worked to suppress slavery. Through a treaty in 1824, he further decreased the power of the Malay nobility; they were forbidden from engaging in any relations with other territories without EEIC consent. Crawfurd offered the Sultan and *Temenggong* a further significant financial reward if they would leave Singapore because he wanted the colony completely free from the ongoing intrigues of Johor-Riau politics and to finalize Britain's hold on Singapore. In case the financial enticements were insufficient for the Sultan and *Temenggong* to leave Singapore, he also sought to make their lives uncomfortable. For example, he ordered the construction of a road through the Sultan's compound. They did not leave, but they were removed from Singapore's governance.

Singapore's first official census occurred in 1824 and stands as testimony to the enormous development of this young colony. There were 11,000 residents that year with the largest population being Malay, then Chinese, then Bugis. Indians comprised the next largest group and then Europeans, mostly British, and even a few Armenians and Arabs. Already, in Singapore's fifth year of modern existence, it was the diverse, globalized society one sees today. Twelve European trading companies, mostly related to the EEIC, had established operations in Singapore by then. Another 1824 landmark achievement was the Anglo-Dutch Treaty of London, through which Singapore became fully and securely a permanent British holding. In exchange for leaving Bengkulu and staying away from Dutch activities south of the Singapore Strait (leaving the Dutch all of today's Indonesia), the Dutch left Melaka and gave over the Malay Peninsula to British influence. The new colony had survived.

SINGAPORE GROWS AS PART OF THE STRAITS SETTLEMENTS

Kolkata's oversight of Singapore soon brought other changes. With the opportunity to develop the Strait of Melaka region, Kolkata decided in 1826 to integrate the three Malay-area colonies, Penang, Melaka, and Singapore, into one administrative unit, the Straits Settlements, with the headquarters in Penang. Administratively, this proved to be disastrous. There was a lack of clarity over roles and levels of authority, provisions for travel between the settlements, and titles. Moreover, in the face of increasing financial pressures for the EEIC, particularly after it lost its exclusive access to trade with China, the company reduced staffing levels, leaving the administrative apparatus understaffed, overworked, unmotivated, and largely ineffective. The administrative problems were heightened by the growth that the

Straits Settlements (particularly Singapore) continued to experience. In 1827 the population had risen by more than 5,000 people from the census just three years earlier to a total of 16,634. By 1840 the population numbered 35,389, and by 1860 it had increased to 81,734.[5] Likewise, Singapore's trade more than tripled between 1830 and the mid-1860s.[6] Thus, as administrative staffing faced drastic cuts, the tasks of the administrators increased significantly. The situation became so grave that the Governor General of India declared in 1859 that the administrative problems were "the greatest evil" in the Straits Settlements.

Despite these problems, Singapore prospered, as indicated by the growth in population and trade. Chinese immigration, as Raffles had anticipated, outstripped other groups and by 1867 comprised 65 percent of the population. They primarily came from southeastern China, many as merchants, but some as agricultural laborers, tin miners in the Malay interior, or craftspeople, such as tailors, carpenters, or goldsmiths. The Malay population likewise grew, although not at the pace of the Chinese. Many of the Orang peoples that comprised a significant portion of Singapore's pre-colonial population were assimilated into the Malay community and added to its numbers. Immigration from India also increased. In 1845 Indians represented 10 percent of the population, but by 1860, they had become the second largest ethnic group in Singapore. Coming primarily from southern India, for a long time these immigrants were mostly young men who intended to return home after earning money as traders or laborers or, for a few, serving in the military. Many of the Chinese, too, did not intend to immigrate permanently to Singapore, planning to work hard, save money, send funds to family in China, and later return home. As often happens with such migrant communities, some return home, but many remain, eventually becoming permanent settlers. Europeans, primarily Britons, also increased in population, although their numbers remained quite low relative to their status and influence. By the 1860s, there had never been more than 500 Europeans at a time in Singapore, although they exclusively staffed the upper levels of the administration and provided much of the capital for trade. The only group that did not experience growth in the first decades of Singapore's administration by the EEIC was the Bugis.[7] With a majority of this population growth occurring due to improving commercial opportunities, it is clear that Singapore's demographic development, creating a diverse ethnic composition that is still present today, was due to the international economic forces of globalization, driven heavily by the colonial activities of the English East India Company and its lucrative trade between China, India, and Europe, with Singapore conveniently positioned in the middle of the eastern half of the commerce route.

In addition to population growth, Singapore received several other boosts in prominence in the 1830s. First, in 1832, Singapore replaced Penang as the capital of the Straits Settlements. The second was due to its strategic location for the military. The Opium Wars (1839–1842 and 1856–1860) were Britain's successful attempts to gain power in China and to reverse its trade imbalance that left, in the minds of the British, too much silver bullion being paid in the direction of China. Britain tried to counter monetary payments by shipping tons of opium produced in Britain's Indian holdings, leading to the growth of extensive opium dens in China, in particular in Guangzhou (formerly Canton). While opium import and use was illegal in Britain due to its harmful effects and addictive nature, the British had no qualms about pushing opium trade in other societies. The opium revenue reversed the imbalance of trade, tipping it in Britain's favor and facilitating the affordable import of Chinese manufactured goods, particularly silk and porcelain, and tea.

The Chinese government banned the import of opium in 1836 and worked hard to eradicate the opium dens. In 1839 Chinese officials in Guangzhou turned back a British merchant ship, and the British responded by sending warships in 1840. The British navy's greater military strength and technology overwhelmed the Chinese, who suffered a profound and humiliating loss. They were forced to sign the Treaty of Nanking, which gave all advantage to the British. Not only were Britons in China not subject to any Chinese laws, Britain was freed of payments to the Chinese imperial administration, gained free access to five ports, claimed control of Hong Kong, and was no longer subject to any trade restrictions with China. As a result, opium imports to China more than doubled in the next 30 years.[8] The Second Opium War began in 1856 after Britain claimed treaty violations in the form of some trade restrictions in the five open ports. The second war resulted in further humiliation for the Chinese and further hastened a decline in imperial power. Because of Singapore's strategic location, it was the departure point and supply center for British naval forces involved in the Opium Wars and thus played a significant role in Britain's successes over China. For the first time, Singapore became an important center for the military operations of the British Empire, which highlighted Singapore's geographic value for British military influence from Southeast Asia to East Asia. Despite that, Britain decided to use its new territory of Hong Kong as its premier naval base in the region.

While population increases, administrative changes, and military strategy all added to Singapore's growing prominence, the most significant change for Singapore, because it drove so many of the other changes, was the expansion of trade through the free port. The nature of Singapore's trade was what is formally called *entrepôt*, which means that little was actually produced in the port area; it was almost solely a transshipment port where goods were brought in from one location, traded in the port, and then shipped out to the purchaser's destination. Singapore was central for the trade between China, India, and Europe; but it was also an important regional entrepôt site for trade (some of it smuggled to avoid Dutch restrictions and fees on goods traded through Singapore) between Thailand and various islands of Indonesia. The most typical commodities were foods, medicines, tea, porcelain, pottery, and silk from China, Vietnam, and Thailand; opium from India; cotton goods and firearms from Britain; and rice, spices, mother-of-pearl, rattan, and camphor from Indonesia. There was relatively little importing done on the west coast of the Malay Peninsula, but the east coast had ports where supplies and opium were brought for colonies of Chinese tin miners and traders in gold, tin, produce, and spices; this more regional trade also went through Singapore.

The growth in trade occurred in an environment of international trade system change, particularly with regard to the English East India Company. Pressures for increased competition led to two acts of the British parliament that incrementally weakened the company, yet ultimately opened other doors for trade. The first, an 1813 act of parliament, even before Singapore's establishment as a colony, ended the EEIC's monopoly on trade between Britain and India. That had been a lucrative special arrangement, and other merchants wanted access and profits. As soon as the monopoly ended, new trading houses, import/export firms independent of the EEIC, grew and moved into the Britain-India market. Similar commercial lobbying pressures arose regarding the China trade, and in 1833 another act of parliament ended the EEIC monopoly with China and EEIC trading activities. The company retained governing functions, but its role as a global economic power was gone, and new trading houses rose up to take its place in commerce. The mercantile community in Singapore, like in other areas once exclusively controlled by the EEIC, formed chambers of commerce to advance their trading interests and influence policies. Singapore's chamber was established in 1837 and, as one example of its activities, joined with other comparable chambers in Indian cities to praise a specific political pressure group, the London East India and China Association. This group successfully lobbied for duties on sugar to be the same whether it came from the East or West Indies and in general represented the local mercantile communities' interests to the British parliament.[9] This dynamic of multiple commercial organizations competing and lobbying is a significant shift from the monopolistic control by the EEIC. By 1846 there were 43 trading houses in Singapore, of which 20 were British, 6 Jewish, 5 Chinese, 5 Arab, 2 Armenian, 2 German, 1 Portuguese, 1 American, and 1 Parsi-Indian.[10] Trade in Singapore was a global endeavor; however, certain groups were especially prominent in certain roles, specifically the British with their capital and the Chinese in exchange. The Chinese were the intermediaries between the British traders and other groups, including fellow Chinese traders as well merchants from other parts of Asia.

While trade grew, it was not considered steady or reliable growth by participants in the merchant community. Singapore was subject to the fickle turns of trading trends that will befall international commerce but particularly in the case of an entrepôt port like Singapore with few local commodities on which to rely. Several practices and events affected Singapore's fate. One was the development of clipper ships, which were extensively used for trade between India and China by the 1830s. These ships, with much more effective sails than earlier vessels, made shipping less dependent on monsoon winds that only allowed seasonal trips between India and China and thus permitted more trips per year. The clipper ships could also travel faster, meaning lesser need to stop at intermediate ports like Singapore to restock supplies. This fundamentally advantaged Britain's opium trade with China, but was not helpful to Singapore.

Moreover, the Dutch, not eager to facilitate British trade and profits, restricted trade from its Indonesian holdings that would transit through Singapore, for example extra fees were charged. With time, the Dutch eased the restrictions, which should have helped Singapore's situation, except the easing of restrictions also opened Dutch-held ports in Indonesia to freer trade. This created greater competition for Singapore because these new ports offered some of the same trade advantages as Singapore, giving merchants more options. Similarly, Singapore's trade was affected by the outcome of the Opium Wars, which produced a boon for Singapore at the time of the wars as a military supply port, but once Britain won access to five ports in China and took complete control of Hong Kong, it created more competition for Singapore and gave merchants still greater options for trade, drawing some away from Singapore. There were various junctures in the decades of the 1830s through the 1850s when Singapore, buffeted by international trade shifts beyond its control, was dismissed as having peaked in its prominence and value as a trade colony. However, all the doomsayers were ultimately proven wrong and, despite the fluctuations, trade grew. In 1824 the value of Singapore's trade was 11 million Spanish dollars (the currency conventionally used for trade in Southeast Asia), but by 1869, the annual value of trade was 89 million Spanish dollars.[11]

Beyond trade, there was one area of significant local economic activity: pepper and gambier farming. These two plants grow together, and by the 1830s, a sizable portion of Singapore's interior was comprised of pepper and gambier plantations. Gambier, a shrub with leaves that are useful in dyeing and tanning leather, was first exported extensively to China, but by the mid-1830s, a European market for the product developed and remained through the rest of the century. Singapore became a regional center for growing and exporting pepper and gambier, and it is estimated that these plantations employed a meaningful portion of Singapore's Chinese laborers by the 1830s.[12] These farming operations were owned by the Chinese, who also controlled much of the unskilled labor coming to Singapore through Chinese secret societies. These major economic spheres of farming and labor, combined with owning the revenue farms for opium and liquor, whose customers were mostly poor laborers, meant that an enormous amount of economic power and wealth became concentrated in the hands of a relatively small number of elites in the Chinese community. That combination of wealthy backers, secret societies, and vice contributed to a number of social ills.

THE DARK SIDES OF EARLY COLONIAL SINGAPORE

Aside from international trade shifts and economic ups and downs, perhaps the biggest threat to Singapore's ever-important trade came from ongoing piracy in the area. Pirates had long thrived in and around Singapore's waters, and a major gathering point for one pirate fleet was just off Singapore's coast, but the problem did not lessen with the region's increase in maritime traffic. This was just too ripe an opportunity for pirates to ignore, and over time, pirates from as far away as China and the Philippines joined local pirate activity around Singapore. By the early 1830s pirates attacked ships just outside the harbor in the middle of the day and moved around the town openly trading in weapons and stolen goods. Legitimate trade along the east coast of the Malay Peninsula was almost brought to a halt, and the Bugis threatened to abandon Singapore as a port unless the piracy could be brought under control. Some of the pirate attacks were large-scale, such as a fight between a 30-boat pirate fleet and boats from the HMS *Southampton* and an EEIC ship. The merchants repeatedly asked for protection because pirates caused considerable losses in a trading system where merchants would normally buy goods on credit and would only recover their money if they were able to sell the goods without loss. However, despite their appeals for help, the merchants were once again in the position of taking the lead where government could not due to lack of funding and restrictions on jurisdiction (captured pirates had to be transported to India to stand trial, for example). In 1832 and 1833 the Chinese merchants banded together to charter vessels, arm them, and patrol the harbor area to try to protect their investments. The difficulty of dealing with the pirates was heightened because of their association and support from the *Temenggong* (by then Ibrahim, son and successor to *Temenggong* Abdul Rahman who held that office at the time of Raffles's arrival), who was profiting from the piracy as had been a tradition in the region for centuries. The government in India finally responded to pleas from the merchants and the local administrators and in 1837 sent the HMS *Wolf* to support the EEIC steamer *Diana*. This was the pirates' first experience with a steamship, which was not at the mercy of the sometimes calm winds of the Strait of Melaka; and the change in strategic advantage alarmed the pirates and their leader, the *Temenggong*, to such a degree that they largely abandoned their operations.

While it is on the surface easy to condemn such activities as simply illegal behavior, it is worthwhile to note that in the local cultures of Southeast Asia, piracy was not considered an obviously criminal or even shameful activity. The Malay nobility considered gaining the financial benefits of piracy to be a right of their station and birth and considered the seas part of their rightful domain. Raffles himself attempted to sway the Sultan and *Temenggong* to engage in commerce rather than supporting piracy and was told quite bluntly that trade was less honorable than raiding ships. Indeed, even outside of the regional context, Europeans and Americans used privateering, a government-authorized seizing of private ships and their cargo by other privately-owned ships, as a wartime strategy and considered it perfectly legitimate if one's own ships were the privateers rather than the targets.

The waters were relatively free of pirates for a time, however, piracy flared up again in the 1850s, primarily from Chinese pirates that were able to prey on larger boats than earlier pirate gangs and pirates from the Mindanao area of the Philippines. This spike in piracy caused an incredible disruption in trade between Singapore and China and southern Vietnam (then known as Cochin China), and as during the earlier wave of pirate activity, Singapore was once again a primary lair for pirates to purchase weapons and sell their booty. What eventually put an end to the second wave of extreme levels of piracy was international cooperation in antipiracy efforts through formal treaties. The British in the areas around the Malay Peninsula, working with the Dutch in Indonesia, the Spaniards in the Philippines, and Chinese in and around China, finally overwhelmed the power of the largest and most effective pirate forces.

In addition to the recurrent scourge of pirates, the vast wealth disparity created troubling conditions for both elites and the masses living in poverty. In general, wealth brought enormous advantages. Life for the wealthy featured frequent outdoor sports activities such as horse racing, cricket, sailing regattas, and other entertainments like dances and dinners. Even better, wealth sheltered people from the diseases that cost many lives of the poor living in crowded slums. However, the elites became concerned about the possibility of an uprising of the poorer peoples of Singapore, and there were decades of discussion by administrators in India and Singapore about the need for some sort of fortification to serve as a refuge for the Europeans living there should an uprising occur and to protect Singapore from potential attack from an enemy. The lack of an obvious enemy left the administration in India slow to act in providing defenses (most of those proposed by Raffles were never built), and it was not until 1859 that Fort Canning was constructed. Such was the location and nature of the fort that it would provide a refuge in the case of local civil unrest, but it would not be especially useful in repelling an enemy attack or even to assure the safety of commerce, particularly as some trade was moving away from the Singapore River area to the deeper natural port, known as New Harbour (today Keppel Harbour), southwest of the city center between the main island of Singapore and the islands of Pulau Brani and Sentosa. The threat of civil unrest was the only thing marring an otherwise luxurious lifestyle.

In contrast, for those with a less privileged existence, life was not as fine. The vast majority of immigrants to Singapore were poor, lacking education and job skills, and above all unmarried and male, creating an unstable, transitory population. Ongoing poverty, malnutrition, overcrowding, and opium abuse were rampant; in 1848, a European doctor concerned with social reform estimated that 20 percent of the adult population of Singapore and more than 50 percent of Chinese adults were addicted to opium.[13] There were some attempts to persuade the administration, the European elite, and wealthy Chinese merchants to take action to stem opium use, highlighting its connection to many health and social problems, but these efforts were dismissed. There were deaths from starvation, and until a wealthy member of the Chinese community, Tan Tock Seng, donated funds for its construction, no hospital existed where poor, common people could seek treatment for widespread cholera, smallpox, and other illnesses. There was nothing of any significance done to address high rates of illiteracy, and Singapore lagged other British territories in that respect as well.

Crime was another social problem, and again the government was not effective in its responses. There were several factors feeding this problem. One was the proliferation of Chinese secret societies, which had grown up in relation to domestic events in China, specifically organized opposition to imperial rule. The societies were linked to kinship networks and regions of origin in China and some of the more prominent ones, such as the Heaven, Earth, and Man Society, or Triad, had thousands of members in Singapore. The societies offered some social benefits and, thus, were left alone by administration officials; in particular, they assisted new immigrants to Singapore, providing them with a support network and helping them find jobs. The societies also addressed disputes within their communities, which was likewise convenient for British officials. However, the secret societies were also linked to considerable violence. There was opposition to Christian conversion and society gangs killed 500 Christians and destroyed 30 agricultural operations (gambier and pepper plantations). The societies were connected to prostitution, human trafficking, and indentured servitude. Gangs of hundreds of secret society members staged regular raids in the city, stealing, destroying property and even killing people. They targeted the Malay community first and foremost but also Indians and Europeans. In 1843, the violence became so severe that non-Chinese merchants had a protest meeting. The government responded and appointed a superintendent of police, Thomas Dunman. Dunman was able to make some improvements and the incidents of violent crime decreased, but the ongoing lack of funds hampered his efforts. In 1854, serious fights broke out between the secret societies, of which there were at least 12 by 1860; and while the worst of the conflict remained within the Chinese community, the open conflict between the societies was nevertheless a concern. It was only after 1857, when Dunman was appointed full-time police commissioner that he was able to make substantial progress in creating a police force that could help provide order.

Another social concern that developed in the 1850s was the presence of high numbers (3,000 by 1857) of convicts, primarily from India, although some also arrived from China and elsewhere. The Dutch in Indonesia also sometimes shipped undesirable persons to Singapore. After 1837, when architect George Drumgold Coleman was put in charge of public works, deported convicts provided inexpensive labor for many public projects, including draining swamps for land reclamation, building roads and government buildings, and later constructing large projects such as Fort Canning and St. Andrew's Cathedral. Initially many of the convicts integrated well into society once their sentences were served, and female convicts, in particular, were sought after as brides in a society where there were extremely few women. However, that ease of transition lessened with time, and it was noted in repeated articles in the newspaper, *Singapore Free Press*, that Singapore had become home to many with a sordid past. In one article from 1851, the paper opined that the Straits Settlements had become, "the common sewer . . . for all the scum and refuse of the populations of nearly the whole British possessions in the east."[14] Connected to the globalized nature of Singaporean society, there developed fear among European immigrants that social unrest in China and India would spill over into Singapore and threaten their lives and well-being. The concerns were heightened by civil war in China against the Manchu imperial rule, which brought in rebels from China after events such as an uprising in Amoy in 1853 and another uprising in 1857 in Kuching that fueled fears of spreading anti-British sentiment. The Indian Rebellion of 1857, when Indian troops mutinied against British rule, caused general colonial alarm and increased fears of more convict deportations to Singapore. Finally, local unrest in 1854 secret society conflicts in the Chinese community and more unrest and riots in 1857 among Chinese and Indians in Singapore over implementation of government policies further fueled worry for many European residents. It was not an accident that this coincided with the construction of Fort Canning.

Most of Singapore's problems during its first decades as a colony were attributable to two sources. The first was a weak administration hampered by financial constraints that left it understaffed and underfunded. There were repeated suggestions to impose various forms of charges to raise revenue from trade, but this was unwaveringly and vehemently opposed by the merchant community that feared losing its competitive advantage of free trade. The supervisory administration in India, facing serious decline itself, was reluctant to invest the sums of money that were needed to fund government programs to provide education, social assistance, and security that would have improved the situation of the masses. Thus progress in this area was left to a large degree to private efforts that only emerged when situations became intolerable. Moreover, one of the biggest sources of revenue for the limited administration was from opium, which also helped create a number of the social ills.

The second source of many of Singapore's problems was the nature of the immigrant society itself. People did not come to Singapore with the intention of putting down roots, building a home and family, and making a new life. Young, single, males came to Singapore to work, earn money, and then go back home. Almost no women were in the early immigrant waves, which made virtually impossible the development of a stable society based on family units, which are extremely important across Asian cultures. Instead, Singapore was like a American frontier town with drugs, poverty, crime, and an anything-goes attitude. It was a climate where the Chinese secret societies, violent, yet useful in providing a sense of connection and support for Chinese immigrants, could thrive. Moreover, Singapore's weak administrative structures also fed the problems of a rootless, lawless society.

Despite all these difficulties, however, Singapore in the first decades of its existence as a British colony managed to thrive in many respects. Population grew despite problems, and trade grew, proving Singapore to be a desirable port of call for traders from all over Asia and as far away as Europe and the United States. The administrative issues, however, gave rise to calls for restructuring the nature of British governance of Singapore and, in 1867, fundamental changes were made.

NOTES

1. Malcolm Murfett et al., *Between Two Oceans* (New York, NY: Marshall Cavendish International, 2004), 54 and C. M. Turnbull, *A History of Singapore, 1819–1988*, 2nd ed. (New York, NY: Oxford University Press, 1989), 5.

2. Turnbull, *History of Singapore*, 15.

3. Raffles quoted in Turnbull, *History of Singapore*, 22.

4. Carl Trocki, *Opium and Empire* (Ithaca, NY: Cornell University Press, 1990), 2.

5. Christopher Tremewan, *The Political Economy of Social Control in Singapore* (New York, NY: St. Martin's, 1994), 7.

6. Turnbull, *History of Singapore*, 35–36.

7. Ibid., 36–38.

8. Richard Hooker, "Ch'ing China: The Opium Wars" (http://www.wsu.edu/~dee/CHING/OPIUM.HTM, 1996).

9. Anthony Webster, "The strategies and limits of gentlemanly capitalism: the London East India agency houses, provincial commercial interests, and the evolution of British economic policy in East and South East Asia, 1800–50," *Economic History Review* 59 (2006): 743–764.

10. Turnbull, *History of Singapore*, 39.

11. Barbara Leitch Lepoer, ed., *Singapore: A Country Study* (Washington, D.C.: Government Printing Office of the Library of Congress, 1989, http://countrystudies.us/singapore/).

12. Carl A. Trocki, *Singapore: Wealth, Power and the Culture of Control* (New York, NY: Routledge, 2006), 22.

13. Turnbull, *History of Singapore*, 63.

14. Ibid., 55.

4

A Crown Colony: 1867–1942

Changing trade practices were a key factor in the administrative development of Singapore. While the English East India Company (EEIC) long controlled trade between Asia and Britain, the EEIC's monopolistic control over that trade had ended, and the company had weakened and was relieved of administrative control of India in 1858. Even before its demise, merchants all over Asia were looking increasingly toward trading houses in London, rather than India, for their business partnerships. This was also facilitated by technological improvements in transportation, specifically the steamship, which allowed for faster communications and trade between Britain and British holdings in Asia. With the end of the EEIC, these stronger direct ties, and the long-term weaknesses of EEIC administration of the Straits Settlements, the British government took direct control of administering Singapore. British colonial authority transformed Singapore in many respects; it grew to greater significance and scale as a trade port, and it experienced major societal changes in the areas of social order and the creation of distinctive identities among the people.

THE END OF ENGLISH EAST INDIA COMPANY CONTROL

There were incremental steps in the transfer of control from Kolkata to London. The Straits Settlements had already been removed from control by the Bengal (India) Presidency in 1851 and had been placed under the authority of a governor-general. This pleased the merchant community, which hoped that better administration would help the colony further increase its thriving trade. However, few beneficial changes actually occurred. Instead, the EEIC's charter was renewed in 1853, and a new legislative council (on which Singapore had no representation) was established. The Council sought to standardize the administration of the various EEIC holdings in the region; and this did not please the Singaporean merchants, who began demanding separation from the EEIC. Merchants in Singapore held public meetings and petition drives to voice various complaints they had with the administration of the legislative council, including not dealing effectively with piracy, the importation of convicts, slow judicial reforms, and the threat of port duties, which Singaporean merchants had long opposed. Poorly handled administrative reforms gave rise to rioting in 1857, which contributed to a climate of concern fed by civil unrest in India and China. The European merchants feared widespread regional opposition to British colonial control, such as it was. In response, they called a public meeting at which they decided to support a petition from the European merchants of Kolkata to the British parliament asking that the EEIC be dissolved, and further, they petitioned that the Straits Settlements be directly ruled by London. The petition, supported only by Singapore within the Straits Settlements, condemned the lack of representation in the ruling bodies of the Straits Settlements and claimed that India had disregarded the wishes and concerns of the Singaporean community. The merchants reiterated specific complaints about piracy, port dues, etc. that had been points of contention for some time.

The result was a 10-year process of negotiations for the transfer of administrative control from India to the British Colonial Office in London. The parliament reacted positively, so success seemed assured, but it did not prove easy to accomplish. Most problematic were financial issues. Estimates of revenue and expenses for administering the Straits Settlements varied widely, leading the British government to worry about the administrative costs. The India Office, having taken over administrative control following the dissolution of the EEIC, had difficulty disentangling the various Straits Settlements-related accounts, leading to further confusion about the financing. Port fees were added in 1863 when the Indian Stamp Act was applied to Singapore. The merchants opposed the fees because they increased the cost of trade, but the fees finally made Singapore self-supporting and alleviated many of the financial concerns of the Colonial Office.

Another major sticking point was how much military protection would be necessary and how costly that would be. Fort Canning had been built in 1860, but necessary staffing levels remained contentious. A shift in interest by the War Office ultimately helped pave the way for a solution. Britain's main military base in East Asia was Hong Kong, but the Admiralty began to reconsider that venue and, in 1866, looked at Singapore as an alternative. The military question was settled with a limited garrison being stationed in Singapore, supported by British primacy on the seas. Finally, a bill was passed in the British parliament, and on April 1, 1867, the Straits Settlements became a crown colony.

ONGOING GROWTH OF TRADE

As was the pattern for much of Singapore's history, the global economy drove many of the changes that occurred after Singapore became a crown colony, including its growth in trade, increase in population, and improvements in social order and stability. The most important developments leading to the dramatic expansion in trade were, first, the rise of the use of steamships and, second, the expansion of British imperial control into the interior of the Malay Peninsula and beyond the port colonies of the three parts of the Straits Settlements.

The Growth of the Steamship

Before the Suez Canal opened in 1869, the Strait of Melaka was geographically advantageous for any trade between East or Southeast Asia and India and potentially onward to Europe. For trade going directly from East or Southeast Asia to Europe, the Strait of Sunda between the Indonesian islands of Sumatra and Java was a more direct route from Asia, around the Cape of Good Hope, and up the west coast of Africa to Europe. However, the opening of the Suez Canal made the Strait of Melaka the shortest route to travel via India to Europe. The distance saved was immense. The trip around the African continent between Mumbai, India, and Liverpool, England, was 11,560 nautical miles; via the Suez Canal, that trip was reduced to 5,777 nautical miles. The total trip from China to Europe was cut by between one-quarter and one-third with the opening of the Canal.[1]

Hand in hand with and, indeed, promoted by the opening of the Canal, was the rise in steamships for global trade. The steamship was not completely new to Southeast Asia—the EEIC's ship *Diana* had been used in fighting pirates in1837; however, as a primary vehicle for shipping, it grew rapidly in popularity with the opening of the Canal. First, the steamship was advantageous in that it did not rely on the annual monsoon winds that had blown ships between Singapore and China and Singapore and India for centuries, thus trade could be conducted year-round. Second, the old, wind-driven clipper ships were not able to use the Suez Canal easily. The cost of towing such a ship through the 100-mile-long Canal was prohibitive, and the Red Sea was difficult for the clipper ships to navigate. Thus, the use of the Suez Canal fell almost exclusively to steamships, which could make their way through the Canal and onward under their own power. The use of the Canal by steamships was so nearly exclusive that between December 1869 and April 1875, only 238 sailing ships traveled through the Canal out of 5,236 total ships.[2]

The coal-powered steamships had one major disadvantage to wind-driven sailing ships: fuel. Ships either had to carry adequate fuel for the voyage, which for a long trip could take up too much valuable cargo space, or have access to regular and reliable refueling stations along the route. The long and relatively less developed coast of Africa was not convenient for such fuel depots, but with the shorter route through the Canal and the developed port system around the Indian Ocean and beyond, the steamships had access to those refueling stations.

Singapore experienced trade growth since its founding as a colony, but it had become somewhat less essential as a Maritime Silk Road trade port after the advent of the clipper ships, which were able to sail all the way from China to India without stopping. The rise of steamships, however, restored Singapore's centrality to trade, as it became an important fueling port for the steamships trading with Europe, China, other parts of Asia, and even North America. By the end of the 1870s, clipper ships had disappeared from the China trade, and all the trade between Asia and Europe relied on coal-powered steamers. British merchants' willingness to shift to the steamship helped assure the continuation of British supremacy in maritime trade and Singapore's increasing role in that.

Expanding Colonization and Growth of Commodities

Trade also grew as colonizing activities increased in the region. The Spaniards increased their activity in the Philippines; the French consolidated control in Indochina (today Vietnam, Cambodia, and Laos); the Dutch in Indonesia shifted their commercial policies to be more open to trade going through Singapore; and the British and other European colonial powers came to agreements, essentially forced on Thailand, that increased access to Thai trade. As a regional trading center, Singapore benefited from the activities of the European empires.

The other major development that increased Singapore's trade was Britain's expansion of control on the Malay Peninsula, accompanied by shifts in global commodity demands. The Malay Peninsula, other than the Straits Settlements, was in the hands of the local, traditional Malay nobility. However, increasingly the Malay interior and Southeast Asia in general, became the source, and Singapore the gathering and distribution point, for various commodities that were exceedingly valuable on the global market. Initially, tin mining was an area of sharp increase in the interior of the Malay Peninsula. Controlled and worked largely by the Chinese, the tin mines created demand for labor from China to deliver the tin that the canning industry, expanded greatly in the United States during the Civil War, needed for production. While the Chinese ran the operations, they did so largely with European financial backing. There was growing unrest in the Malay Peninsula, fed in part by tensions with the local rulers who had little authority over the newly arriving Chinese workers and in part by rivalries between the various Chinese secret societies whose members were the workers. This caused significant concern among business people from both Chinese and European communities in Singapore who wanted better government protection for their investments. Thus began the pressure on the British Colonial Office to increase its control over additional territory in the Malay Peninsula. These demands were, in fact, much more on the minds of local businesspeople by the time Singapore became a crown colony, since their earlier concerns about piracy and the like had largely been remedied. Protection of investments in Malaysia was now high on the agenda for action.

Initially, these demands were not well received by the Colonial Office, which was little interested in the further investment of resources that control of greater territory would require. The British position was made clear in an 1868 communication to the Straits Settlements' Governor, Sir Henry St. George Ord, from the British Secretary of State, "The policy of her Majesty's government in the Malayan peninsula is not one of intervention in native affairs. . . . If merchants or others penetrate disturbed and semi-barbarous independent states . . . they must not anticipate that the British government will intervene to enforce their contracts."[3]

The situation continued to worsen and, in 1873, Singapore-based Chinese merchants made a formal petition to the Colonial Office in London to increase British control on the Peninsula. Governor Ord supported the petition, and the government, motivated in part by concern that other colonial powers in the region may intervene if they did not, decided to act. They forced agreements on the local sultans of what became the Federated States of Malaya and the Unfederated States, initially providing advisors for the Malay rulers and then later consolidating greater direct control.

Ultimately, this proved a lucrative step for the British because within a short time technological advancements and increasing demand in the global commodities markets made the resources they gained from the Malay Peninsula more valuable than ever. While tin mining had been primarily controlled by the Chinese with European financial backing, the advent of steam dredging and other advances led to greater mechanization in mining. Mechanization left mining companies less reliant on Chinese labor, and thus with the Europeans' ability to invest in greater mechanization, the Chinese lost much of their power in the tin mining industry.

The other transformational technological advances affecting the commodities from the Malay Peninsula were in the area of rubber. In 1844, American Charles Goodyear received a patent for the process of vulcanizing rubber. Vulcanization involved heating the raw rubber to remove the sulfur, which left the rubber viable for industrial use. It retained its elasticity and also became weatherproof so that it did not melt in the heat of summer or become brittle in the cold of winter. The demand for vulcanized rubber spiked precipitously with Henry Ford's invention of the automobile assembly line because rubber was needed for the tires of the masses of automobiles that flooded the American and then world markets. In the 1890s, rubber was extensively planted on the Malay Peninsula, and by 1907, there was a commercial plantation in Singapore. The demand for Malay rubber, mostly exported from Singapore, grew from 104 tons in 1905 to 196,000 tons in 1914, which was more than half of the world's rubber supply.[4] Major corporations from Europe and North America, including Dunlop, Goodrich, Goodyear, and Firestone, invested in plantations and rubber production. Most of their operations were on the Malay Peninsula, but they based their operational headquarters primarily in Singapore, which was also the center for export. Oil was a third commodity that was shipped in significant volume through Singapore, coming from oilfields in nearby Sarawak, Sumatra, and Borneo in present-day Malaysia and Indonesia. The growing auto industry fed demand for petroleum, in addition to the rubber.

Singapore's trade in these years shifted from a finished-goods-based market of porcelain, tea, fabrics, and weapons, as it was in the early years of the colony's trade, to a commodities marketplace of raw rubber and unprocessed tin. There was very little industrialization in Singapore or in Malaysia. A few tin smelting and rubber processing factories were built, but mostly the commodities were shipped as raw materials. In the long run, this likely contributed to the low level of industrialization that Singapore faced decades later at its independence.

Shifting Trade Patterns amid the Growth

The overall increased volume of trade during this period was dramatic. The demands of the global market through the new technological developments of canning and automobiles increased the amount of trade but so too did international events. World War I led to further demand for rubber, tin, and petroleum, and Singapore benefited in trade from that as well. Singapore already ranked as the world's seventh largest port in terms of tonnage in 1903.[5] Singapore's trade rose from $11.6 million in 1824 to $147.4 million in 1883 to $975.7 million in 1923 and reached a high in 1926 when the value of trade reached $1.867 billion.[6] In the mid-1920s, rubber comprised just over half of the exports from the Malay Peninsula, and tin comprised another 17.4 percent.[7] The orientation of trade also shifted with the European markets becoming secondary to North American markets. From 1915 onward, except during the worst of the Great Depression, more than 50 percent of Singapore's trade with western countries went to North America. The nature of Singapore's position as an entrepôt left it especially vulnerable to shifts in global demand. Thus, the worldwide Great Depression that began in 1929 and continued into the 1930s deeply and negatively affected Singapore's trade. Demand for commodities fell as production and demand for finished goods fell. In turn, the prices for commodities fell. For example, the cost of rubber on the London markets dropped by 75 percent during the Depression. The value of tin faced a similar drop. By 1933, the value of Singapore's trade had declined to $512.8 million, and it took until the 1950s to recover to the peak of the 1920s.[8]

While trade prospered with some fluctuations during the decades after the Colonial Office took control, structural changes in the economy led to a number of other significant developments in Singapore's globalized economy. A significant shift was a move away from the simple transshipment trade activity. The actors remained constant, but their activities changed in response to new challenges and opportunities. For the European community, the increasing mechanization of tin and the growth of the rubber industry, worked primarily by low-cost laborers from India, left them in a stronger position relative to the Chinese merchant community who no longer dominated in terms of providing inexpensive labor from China and running mining operations. This was a shift from past economic relationships between the two groups.

Since the beginning of British trade in Singapore, British agency houses dominated local trade and then expanded into global trade, acting as intermediaries between the global markets and Southeast Asian goods. Initially, they provided capital to Chinese intermediaries by giving them European goods on credit. This served as capital for the Chinese who, possessing both language skills and networks, then traded them for local or Chinese goods that then went back to the British creditors. The agency houses initially simply received a commission on these trade deals. This pattern of bartered trade continued into the twentieth century. With time and growth in prominence and wealth, however, the agency houses expanded their activities beyond simple trade. They began offering shipping services, banking services, shipping insurance, and commercial information. Major financial organizations of today, such as Barclay's Bank or Hong Kong and Shanghai Bank (HSB) have roots in these activities of the agency houses of Singapore. The agency houses also undertook major business projects, such as the creation of Tanjong Pagar Dock Company, which expanded Singapore's port facilities in the 1870s, or the Straits Steamship Company, created in 1890 to break the monopoly of European-based shipping companies servicing Singapore's shipping needs. Historian Carl Trocki described the agency houses as, ". . . the key 'agents of change' that created the empire and forged the global economy."[9]

The Chinese merchant community also underwent significant changes during this time of shifting economic activities. They mostly retained their role as middlemen for trading and amassed considerable wealth, yet economic activity did not remain constant for them. By the time Singapore became a crown colony, many Chinese merchants, rather than sending their money back to family in China, began investing their considerable wealth in business endeavors in Singapore. This included, in particular, plantations in the rural areas of Singapore where pepper and gambier, used for tanning leather, were cultivated together. Unskilled Chinese laborers, imported to Singapore through Chinese agents, worked the production. In trade, the Chinese merchants developed extensive networks throughout

Southeast Asia that became the basis for later commercial operations. Their wealth and prominence was significant, especially given the number of Chinese people in Singapore relative to a small number of Europeans, whose power in governance and economics was somewhat diluted by how few there were. In fact, Rudyard Kipling noted upon visiting Singapore, "England is by the uninformed supposed to own the island."[10]

However, several factors eventually motivated wealthy Chinese businesspeople to broaden the scope of their business activities. Shifts in the network of unskilled Chinese labor supply, changes in production activities in the western-controlled Malay tin mines, a decline in the gambier and pepper plantations in Singapore proper, and finally even the onset of the Great Depression led to the changes. The development of a Chinese banking system was among the most significant of the new undertakings, and some of these institutions form the basis for major Singaporean banks today, like the Oversea-Chinese Banking Corporation (OCBC Bank).

Finally, it is worth noting that Singapore's economy was repeatedly buffeted by economic ups and downs during this period. This too shaped economic behaviors and may have driven the creation of new or expanded financial institutions beyond investments in trade or land. As integrated into the global economy as Singapore was, its fortunes were tied to economic cycles. For example, the World War I era was a boom time for the commodities exports, so Singapore fared very well. However, after the war, as the global economy reoriented to peacetime, there was a downturn, and commodity prices fell. From February to December 1920, rubber prices fell from one dollar and 15 cents to 30 cents per pound. Tin prices dropped by more than 60 percent during the same period.[11] Trade rebounded through the 1920s, driven mostly by increased automobile demand, yet fell off again during the Great Depression. Overall commodity prices had a downward trend due in large part to increasing, and sometimes over, supply. In the early part of the century, the price of rubber from the Peninsula averaged 68 British pence per pound. From 1910 to 1919, the average price was down to 44 pence per pound, despite wartime demand. In the 1920s, the average price of rubber was 17 pence per pound, and during the 1930s it was down to a mere 6 pence per pound average.[12]

There were various attempts to stabilize the economy. The administration enacted currency reform as early as 1903, pegging the value of the new Straits dollar to the British pound, which helped make currency values less volatile and increased economic stability.

In dealing with commodity price fluctuations, the government implemented several protectionist trade policies during the Depression years, including international agreements to limit rubber and tin production to keep prices high. Furthermore, the British government introduced imperial preference tariffs that were designed to protect British markets from foreign goods. The tariff scheme was structured so that goods produced in Britain received the most protection, since they were not subject to tariffs, which raised the cost of a product. Goods produced in the British Empire, including Singapore and Malaysia, had tariffs placed on them but at a lower rate than goods produced outside the Empire; thus goods imported to Britain via Singapore were more expensive to British consumers than goods produced at home but were less expensive than goods produced outside of British control, such as rubber from Dutch-held Indonesia.

SOCIETAL CHANGES IN A GLOBALIZED ECONOMY

Such significant shifts in the economic activity of Singapore led to corresponding shifts in society. One of the most notable was the steadily increasing levels of immigration that occurred during Singapore's early years as a crown colony. The increased British control of the Malay Peninsula combined with the increased commodity demands made Singapore, as the gateway to the Malay Peninsula, an attractive destination for labor migration. Factors as varied as poverty, civil unrest (particularly in China), natural disasters, exploitation by landlords, and overpopulation in rural areas encouraged workers by the thousands to leave their home countries, especially China and India. In 1871, Singapore had a population of 97,111 of which almost 54,600 were Chinese, 26,000 were Malay, 11,600 were Indian, and only 1946 were European. By 1931, the total population had grown to 557,745, of which there were 418,600 Chinese, 65,000 Malays, 50,800 Indians, and 8,100 Europeans.[13]

While many immigrants remained in Singapore, most of them continued onward to the Malay Peninsula or sometimes present-day Indonesia. In the vast majority of cases, these workers anticipated returning home after earning some money. However, for a variety of reasons, many found it difficult to save the money they had hoped, and they remained.

Labor Migration

Indians came in larger numbers once the rubber industry developed on the Malay Peninsula. There were several programs to import Indian workers that were at least somewhat regulated by Britain's

India Office. Until about 1900 the chief means by which Indian workers came to Singapore and onward was through indenture contracts. There were formal recruiters who assisted in the process, and workers had to agree to pay back from their wages the cost of their travel and any recruitment costs. The average contract was for one to three years; however, since wages were so low, workers often stayed indentured longer. If the contract was broken, it was considered a criminal offense. With time, the *kangani* system developed. A *kangani* was a well-known Indian laborer who would contract with, supervise, and discipline workers and would act as an intermediary between plantation owners and the laborers. The *kangani* would not, however, be responsible for the workers' living or eating arrangements. The shift between indentured and *kangani*-assisted migration happened toward the end of the nineteenth century, with the majority of migrant Indians coming through the *kangani* system by 1905. This system reached its peak from 1910–1919 when 50,000 to 80,000 Indian workers came each year.[14] While much of this Indian labor ultimately went to the Malay Peninsula, by late in the 1800s, increasing numbers of Indian immigrants remained in Singapore. Some were merchants or clerks, but many also worked in hard labor because the Indian community had a near monopoly on transportation-related work: dockworkers, river boatmen, haulers, and the like. What was of long-lasting social significance in the *kangani* system was that women eventually became part of the immigrant labor force, resulting in family unification, permanent settlement, and locally born children. With time, this helped address the gender imbalance within the Indian community in Malaysia and Singapore, which may have increased social stability.

For the Chinese community, the numbers were greater, although the means of recruiting migrant workers bore some similarities to the pre-*kangani* Indian system. Until 1893, emigration from China was officially banned. It is evident that the ban was not enforced, but it hindered formal labor recruitment programs with government involvement such as those that existed in India. In some cases, recruiters tapping into kinship or hometown networks arranged transit, with the costs of the transportation and related expenses being backed by family or friends. In most cases, however, an indenture approach was used. Labor brokers, agencies, or ship captains initially paid a person's expenses for going to Singapore. Local employers then paid back the transit expenses on the workers' behalf, and workers became indentured to Singaporean Chinese businesspeople until such time as their debt (often inflated) could be paid off. Thousands of people came to Singapore using this system.

Social Problems

The indenture approach for poor, unskilled immigrants was often an abusive system associated with many social ills. Most scholars point to the fact that almost all of these Chinese immigrants were men, creating a nearly all-male society, as a factor that sharply exacerbated the social problems of the time. These social problems included poor labor conditions, high levels of opium use, prostitution, and the activities of Chinese secret societies. However, while various social ills were widespread, significant progress was made, especially in the 1900s, toward lessening the problems as part of the social changes that occurred.

Poor Labor Conditions

The indenture contracts left immigrant workers virtual slaves. Not only did they owe their employer for their passage from China and recruitment costs, but they often lived in overpriced, overcrowded, employer-owned, low-quality housing that, coupled with other living expenses, left them in abject poverty. The majority of workers came to Singapore with the intention of returning home, but very few were actually able to save enough money to do so. A government study done in 1875 confirmed the poor conditions for so many of Singapore's workers and, in 1877, a new government office was formed, the Chinese Protectorate. There was little opposition to this among economic leaders because it was widely known how bad the situation was for most unskilled workers. The first person to hold the position of Protector was William Pickering, the first European official able to speak several of the Chinese dialects common in Singapore. He first turned his attention toward the abuses of the indenture system by regulating the recruitment agencies that brought workers to Singapore. The next step was to legalize the boarding of ships by Protectorate staff so that workers whose passage had been paid could be released, and those who had to pay for their passage could be taken directly to government offices where their indenture contracts could be officially registered with the Protectorate. This did not end labor abuses completely, but it was a step toward improving the situation for workers. With time, other positive developments were implemented. In 1914, indentured labor from China was banned; and in the 1920s, a series of new labor laws further improved workers' positions, such as the right to bring wage disputes to the Protectorate without cost to the worker. However, the unskilled workers in Singapore continued to face extremely high levels of poverty for all their hard work as rickshaw pullers, stevedores, coal haulers, boatmen, and other menial jobs.

Opium

What exacerbated the poor living conditions of many poor and unskilled workers was opium use. Opium used was blamed for much illness and mortality, but discouraging its use was problematic. The two most powerful groups in Singaporean society, the Europeans and wealthy Chinese merchants, both benefited considerably from the sale of opium. From the earliest decades of the colony, revenue from opium sales and rent (regular payments to the government from those selling the opium) provided a significant portion of the government's funds—up to 60 percent. Wealthy Chinese businesspeople, often in syndicates, owned the opium-selling revenue farms that the government auctioned off to them and benefited from opium sales as well. Thus, incentives were minimal for limiting opium use. Estimates based on anecdotal evidence suggest that as many as 60 to 70 percent of unskilled, and even skilled, Chinese workers were steady opium users, if not addicts.[15] The high levels of opium use worsened the poverty and living conditions of many of the poor workers, in particular. The meager funds they had left after paying their indenture payments, housing fees, and food costs, were often spent on opium to help dull the physical and psychological suffering resulting from hard, physical labor far from home and family, in poor working and living conditions. Between the government's interest in opium profits and the interconnected interests of the wealthy Chinese community who owned the labor contracts of the workers in their businesses who smoked their opium, there was little impetus for change.

In the early decades of the 1900s, however, attitudes began shifting, despite the economic incentives against it. Increasingly, wealthy Singaporeans, especially the Chinese born in the Straits Settlements, sent their sons to Europe for university education. When these young professionals started returning in meaningful numbers, their changed attitudes began shaping Singaporean society. While still holding true to their ethnic identities, they nevertheless were shaped by the cultural norms they encountered in Europe, including an opposition to opium, which had been outlawed in Britain in 1868 when the Pharmacy Act prohibited its sale to all but licensed pharmacists. There was also grassroots pressure in Britain against the Asian-targeted opium trade as part of the larger temperance movement. The Singapore Anti-Opium Society was formed in 1906; and in 1907, due to Colonial Office insistence, the Singaporean administration convened a commission to examine the issue. The commission's findings indicated that opium use was a harmless habit among the rich but was more injurious to the poor because they were only able to afford the dregs of used opium, and it was only a few people, mostly rickshaw pullers, who were actually addicted. As a compromise between the competing pressures of financial incentives versus physical harm, the government took control of opium production in Singapore in 1910. The government manufactured and sold quality opium and then purchased and destroyed the opium waste. This limited the worst of the abuses, and the percentage of government revenue from opium sales fell gradually. By 1934, only 25 percent of revenue came from opium, although the government continued to produce it until World War II.[16]

Prostitution

Another social ill, linked to the poverty of the unskilled workers and the scarcity of women in Singapore, was prostitution. For many workers, extra funds that were not spent on living expenses, indenture payments, or opium were spent on prostitutes. As an illustration of the gender imbalance that fed the problem, in 1884, there were 60,000 Chinese men in Singapore and only 6,600 Chinese women, of which it was estimated that at least 2,000 were prostitutes. In the late 1870s, it was estimated that 80 percent of the females coming to Singapore from China were sold into prostitution.[17] Many had not come voluntarily; some were kidnapped, some were tricked, and others were sold by their families. The Chinese Protectorate did not attempt to stop prostitution but instead sought to prevent women and girls from being forced into prostitution and otherwise abused. The Protectorate was able to mandate the registration of brothels and prostitutes to help regulate the trade. An Office to Protect Virtue was also formed and its staff worked with advisors from the Chinese community to help Chinese women and girls who were unwillingly involved in prostitution. As with increasing social order in other areas, there were improvements with time. In 1914, the sale of women and girls for prostitution was banned; in 1927, the importation of women and girls for prostitution was banned; and then finally in 1930, brothels were banned, although prostitution remained legal. A balancing of the gender ratio may have helped the situation somewhat. The number of women in the Chinese community increased steadily from 1880 onward; increases in female Chinese migration to Singapore varied depending on dialect group, but by the 1930s, there were higher levels of female migration, and the community gained more social stability. In terms of overall population in Singapore, by 1931 there were

205,600 women and 352,000 men.[18] This was still not balanced, but it was much closer than it had been since the colony was founded.

Secret Societies

Finally, there were important changes relating to the Chinese secret societies. The benefits of the secret societies, specifically assistance and support for new immigrants, did not outweigh the problems associated with the groups. There were regular waves of rioting by the societies that resulted in social instability. Moreover, with the increased Chinese immigration to work in the tin mines in Malaysia, almost all of which passed through Singapore, there was a sharp increase in professional thugs (*samseng*) hired to act as enforcers in rougher areas. These thugs were affiliated with the secret societies, which were involved with supplying labor. There were even organized kidnappings assisted by the *samseng* to supply workers for the areas, such as Sumatra, where the working conditions were so poor that few workers would go voluntarily. With more secret society rioting in 1872, the government saw the need to address this problem and, after discussing different approaches, including a law to regulate Chinese immigration (much opposed by the community who wanted to continue the policy of free immigration along with free trade), the government turned over the problem to the Chinese Protectorate.

The Protectorate sought to take over some of the beneficial roles in the community that the secret societies provided, thus reducing their value to the Chinese community, in particular adjudicating financial and domestic disagreements. The Protectorate also attempted to convert some of the secret society leadership into government workers, which would help give the government a bigger presence in the Chinese community. Ultimately, the Protectorate's greatest success came through cutting the interconnections between the secret societies with the opium revenue farms, the supply of labor for plantations, and smuggling. This was done, in part, by the government opening bidding on the opium revenue farms to entrepreneurs from outside Singapore, which introduced more competition and helped break the secret society control of this lucrative industry. When new and different economic opportunities opened to the Chinese community, power within the community shifted to a different set of Chinese organizations: *bangs* or groups based on dialect group and region of origin in China. The *bangs* were led by the wealthy elites from each dialect group, but the *bangs* also incorporated poorer community members;

the leaders were recognized by the government as community representatives.

With the secret societies in decline, it was easier for the government to pass legislation that banned the secret societies. Initially the Protectorate did not wish to go as far as a ban, but Governor Cecil Clementi-Smith, with the support of the Colonial Office, managed to gain adequate public support and pushed it through. The ban did not completely eradicate the secret societies. During economic downswings, the secret societies thrived, but their activities were, and remained, severely reduced from their heyday when they were connected to the lucrative business of opium and labor. Ultimately, they were left to engage in gambling, prostitution, minor smuggling, protection rackets, and other forms of extortion. However, they were never again connected closely to the power holders in Singaporean Chinese society, and the recurrent rioting that had long-plagued Singapore virtually ended.

Overall, during this time period major societal transformations resulted in a larger population and a more orderly society. Policing became more efficient; the Protectorate was created. Many of the changes, for example measures to reduce opium addiction and provide protection for women and girls against involuntary prostitution, were clearly to the social good. What is evident, however, is the demise of a hands-off approach to governance that characterized the early decades of British authority in Singapore and a shift toward governance with a heavier, more controlling hand.

THE DEVELOPMENT OF GROUP IDENTITY

Identities, or how people think of themselves, often matter little until something important is at stake. What transpired in Singapore in the later part of the nineteenth and early twentieth centuries was the beginning of important definitions of social group identities. Initially in Singapore, when most everyone considered themselves temporary residents who would work for a time and then return home, advantages or disadvantages relating to identities could perhaps be more easily dismissed, but when people began establishing themselves as long-term or permanent inhabitants of Singapore, some of those perceptions changed. The process of identity formation and its resulting political significance were wrought by a variety of forces. Globalization, which had shaped so much in Singapore, likewise affected identities. Other developments that formed identities were more internal to society and the government that administered it.

Even without these forces, the foundations for each identity were complex. Within the Chinese community, there were the five major dialect and regional groups that corresponded to the *bangs*; there were class divisions and whether one was born in the Straits Settlements (Straits-Chinese) or born in China. In the Indian community, there were likewise many divisions, the most significant being wealth and area of origin in India, which also shaped language, although the majority spoke Tamil. Even the indigenous people, the Malays, were more diverse than one might expect. The Malay cultural space is much larger than simply the Malay Peninsula and nearby islands like Singapore; it also includes the Indonesian archipelago and beyond. The cultural patterns across the region bore important similarities, including considerable trade and intermingling, thus in the Malay cultural space, the question of who was an insider and who was not was unclear. Non-Malays, particularly the British, lumped together groups like the Bugis and others from Indonesia, although there were some differences among groups. Despite all these divisions within Singapore's ethnic communities, this period also saw the foundations for a Singaporean identity that provided connectivity across the ethnic communal lines, at least for some members of society.

Globalization and Identity

The globalization-related forces that helped shape Singaporeans' identities were largely twofold. First, there were influences from Europe acting on the Asian communities, initially mainly the Chinese community, through Straits-born Asians who sought higher education in Britain. While there, they were influenced by European attitudes and then returned to become prominent leaders in their communities, especially the Straits-Chinese and Indian communities. As mentioned above, these individuals led the way in the anti-opium movement, but they also became advocates for better local education. This experience of European education also strongly contributed to a distinctive Straits-Chinese identity that differed from the identity of immigrant Chinese Singaporeans, who remained more strongly oriented toward China.

The other main globalization-related force working on identities was ideological in nature. While Singaporean Indians were not spurred to anti-British or anticolonial action, they were nevertheless aware of the Indian Independence Movement and Mahatma Gandhi's opposition to policies of racial exclusion and oppression. These racist policies were also in place in other British colonies, including

Singapore, and the ideology of the Indian Independence Movement heightened the awareness of Singaporean Indians to their group status within a discriminatory system.

While globalization of ideology made Indians aware, it mobilized Chinese Singaporeans. China was undergoing major changes in the early decades of the twentieth century, including an anti-imperial struggle that brought an end to two millennia of imperial dynasties. The Nationalists (*Guomindang*) under Sun Yat-sen took control for a time after imperial rule was abolished but struggled for power, and there was soon a competition for leadership between two ideological groups, the Communists and the *Guomindang*. Both of these ideological movements targeted "overseas Chinese" or ethnic Chinese communities outside of China, including those in Singapore, seeking financial and other support.

The political developments and appeals were of great interest to immigrant Chinese in Singapore, who, despite having been in Singapore for a long time, still felt close cultural and emotional ties to home. Political activism in response to events relating to China became common. In 1905, after the United States passed the Exclusion Act against Chinese immigration, many Singaporean Chinese boycotted imports from the United States. A similar boycott against Japanese goods occurred in 1908 after a dispute arose between Japan and China. Leaders in China encouraged Chinese nationalism that included overseas Chinese communities. They encouraged the building of schools, and Singaporean Chinese fell in line with the establishment of additional schools in which Chinese was the language of instruction. Many of these schools used materials imported from China, which helped promote the nationalist message. The Chinese government also advocated the use of standard Mandarin Chinese, the official language of China, as the language of instruction, rather than the varied dialects commonly used within the Chinese community. By 1935, Mandarin Chinese was adopted by all Chinese-medium schools in Singapore. The orientation toward China was strengthened further in the immigrant community by the fact that all of those who could afford it sent their children, products of the Chinese-medium schools, to college in China. This helped spread the Chinese ideologies on the students' return and maintained strong ties into the next generation between China and the overseas immigrant Chinese and their sons.

The schools promoted Chinese nationalism not only through the curricular materials from China but also through a new type of Chinese immigrant. For the first time, intellectuals immigrated to Singapore to flee the ideological struggle taking place and found jobs through which they could spread Chinese viewpoints. Many became teachers in the Chinese-medium schools, some became journalists, and others worked as labor union organizers. This became a concern for the British administration after intense anti-Japanese sentiments developed in Singapore in the 1920s, coinciding with heightened conflict between China and Japan, and led to more civil unrest. Japanese immigrants to Singapore were specifically targeted for harassment. Viewing the schools as a big part of the problem, the government placed restrictions on school materials from China. The government also censored the Chinese-language press, banned the local branch of the *Guomindang*, and made direct efforts against the spread of ideas from the Chinese Communist Party. These policies angered the Chinese community, because they were seen as an identity-related assault on the community itself.

The common focus on China's political events, the introduction of Mandarin Chinese as the universal language of instruction in Chinese-medium schools, and the common alienation caused by the response of the government to the spread of ideologies from China led to greater cohesion within the Chinese immigrant community. The different *bangs* were still present, but ties that formed the basis of a communal identity began to surface. This uniting of interest was also expressed in the business sphere where the most influential businessmen of the immigrant Chinese community founded the Singapore Chinese Chamber of Commerce in 1906 after they were no longer welcome in the European-dominated Singapore Chamber of Commerce.

These new-found connections across the *bangs*, however, did not extend to the Straits-Chinese. Most Straits-Chinese were not interested in the internal affairs of China. In addition, they were likely to have been educated in English-medium schools, which contributed to a significant division between Straits-born Chinese and immigrant Chinese. Instead of focusing on China's politics, they were more interested in social and educational issues in Singapore. They organized the Social Purity Union, the Boy Scouts, and the Singapore Volunteers. They even had their own business association, the Straits-Chinese British Association, an alternative to the Singapore Chinese Chamber of Commerce of the immigrant Chinese community.

The Singaporean Malay community also had some experience with ideological globalization that also helped crystallize their identity. Considering again that the Malay cultural space extends across Indonesia, some Singaporean Malays were taken with calls for an Indonesian nation in what was still the Dutch East Indies. Others found resonance in pan-Islamic movements. Neither of these had significant effects on the Malay community as a whole; instead, the Malay identity was more influenced by various internal events that also shaped the other communal identities.

Internal Factors and Identity

In terms of internal factors encouraging identity development, education proved to be a point of ongoing contention and a rallying point. Education was not provided in any sort of coherent way; there were multiple school systems, supported financially by different entities, with varying educational content. Given the lack of a cohesive approach, the quality of education differed greatly. The government changed its policies on subsidizing schools time and again, depending the economic climate or political atmosphere. Basic education tended to receive government support more consistently than secondary education, and Malay- and English-medium schools tended to be funded more consistently than schools where the teaching was provided in Chinese or Tamil. Government financial assistance, however, was not necessarily an indicator of quality of education, because the Malay-medium schools were of notoriously poor quality. Malays were seen as being destined to do menial tasks, so there was little attention paid to providing a good education. Tamil-medium schools were similar. Chinese-medium schools, however, developed along a very different trajectory. Many wealthy members of the Chinese community wanted to be seen as philanthropists, so in addition to helping fund hospitals and other public works, they also funded schools for members of their particular dialect groups. The schools had mixed outcomes, although overall, they were better than Malay or Tamil schools. English-medium schools tended to be good, partly because the government had an interest in educating elite members of the local communities to a level where they could serve as clerks or similar jobs where English was needed.

The greatest advantage fell to those in English-medium schools, most frequently attended by wealthy Chinese, particularly Straits-Chinese. As access to those schools was limited by wealth and other factors, this approach to education heightened class, ethnic, culture, and language differences between the communities, and raised people's consciousness of those differences and the reasons for them. The Malays, in particular, had limited opportunities for social mobility; most were illiterate or were educated minimally in the poor Malay schools. In their efforts at commerce, they came head to head with tough Chinese competition and typically did not fare well. These problems gave much greater significance to being Malay and what made it distinctive among the various cultures of Singapore: the language and religion.

The Malay community, as indigenous inhabitants, had an identity of "sons of the soil;" this is perhaps also because they, more than the other communities, managed to retain a fairly traditional lifestyle outside of the urban area and thus had concerns about maintaining their group's claim to the land. Moreover, by the 1920s, the Malays felt further threatened by the growing influence of the Straits-Chinese. In 1926, the first Malay political organization was created. The Singapore Malay Union sought to protect Malay interests relative to the Chinese community, but of greatest concern were the problems relating to the poor quality of Malay education. This group became an important voice for the interests of the Malay identity group.

Various policies implemented by the government to increase social order also fed the distinctions between groups in Singaporean society. Some of the policies of the decreasingly hands-off administration may have appeared beneficial on the surface, and indeed were likely intended as such but, in fact, indicated an increasing disconnect between the small number of elite Europeans who governed Singapore and the masses of Asians who comprised the population. There were some initiatives to connect the government more closely to the communities; for example, the administration created a Chinese Advisory Board to provide a formal tie between the government and the largest of Singapore's ethnic communities. However, there were many policies that gave the Asians of Singapore a different outlook.

In the 1870s the British administration decided to address the densely constructed Asian neighborhoods packed with "shophouses" that were usually three stories high, were backed up onto one another with no rear access, and were next to one another with little or no space in between. They also had covered sidewalks at the front where retail, storage, or even living space spilled out into the sidewalks and streets. The government wanted to improve sanitation by installing sewer and drainage systems, which helped with severe public health problems like the continuous outbreaks of cholera. In order to do this and to enhance efforts to reduce crime, the government decided to open up these areas that were both people's homes and businesses, which meant removing entire buildings. To the Asian population, this seemed to be an assault on their property and living space.

To make matters worse, in the interest of improving traffic flow for larger vehicles, the government also sought to ban sidewalk space for storage or commercial use. This appeared as a further attack on property and even on aspects of people's daily lives and financial well-being, because many would buy their food and other basic provisions from street sellers (known as hawkers) who operated on the sidewalks and earned their income through those street sales. This gave rise to the Verandah Riots as people sought to defend their right to use the sidewalks. The government used Chinese community leaders to try to explain its intent, but these policies nevertheless gave rise to tensions and were an indicator of a serious division between the Europeans charged with running Singapore and the Asian masses who lived there.

The government's actions into the 1920s were also seen as disruptive and even blatantly discriminatory as it sought to address other political concerns. Again, the intervention in Chinese-medium schools to restrict the spread of Chinese nationalism and the censorship of the Chinese-language press were poorly received in the Chinese community. To make it worse, as the Great Depression negatively affected Singapore's economy, the government introduced, for the first time, restrictions, in the form of a quota system, on immigration of unskilled male workers, which gravely affected Chinese immigration. In 1930, 242,000 Chinese immigrants were allowed; in 1931 that number dropped to less than 28,000, and in 1931, the quotas for Chinese immigrants were reduced even more.[19] In 1933, the Aliens Ordinance, which combined quotas with fees that immigrants had to pay on arrival in Singapore, replaced the existing quota system. Since this law did not apply to British subjects, it left not only Europeans but also Indians untouched and was thus clearly targeted against Chinese immigrants. The Chinese saw the immigration restrictions as plainly discriminatory. These immigration policies, combined with other policies viewed as offensive, led to an unprecedented increase in racial tensions.

The resentment against these laws and policies was further fed by blatant racism on the part of the British. In part it was an issue of general attitude. British colonizers were concerned with keeping up appearances to underscore their perceived superiority to the Asian communities and, thus, were never willing to be seen doing work that could be considered menial. However, as more Asians from Singapore were educated in Britain and saw the poor living and working conditions of many Britons, they gained perspectives on the realities of British and European society and realized that Caucasians were not inherently superior.

This new awareness coincided with increasingly discriminatory policies on important issues like employment. The British practiced policies of racial exclusion in Singapore like in other parts of the British Empire. Educated Asians could gain employment in the Civil Service, the Medical Service, and the Legal Service, but they could not gain promotion out of the lowest levels. With their British educations, they worked in professional positions with Britons who were sometimes less qualified or less capable than they were, but the Asians could not be promoted. This happened even in the face of colonial administrators who stayed in Singapore for shorter stints and thus had less familiarity with the community, and with fewer such administrators knowing local languages. Compounding these barriers to promotion were dual pay scales in which Europeans received higher pay than Asians for comparable work. These European-educated Singaporeans had learned the English language, and they had been socialized to dress like Europeans and enjoy European sports and activities, which were part of the British attempt to "civilize" the Asian communities. However, just as they were becoming more Europeanized, they were denied most of the advantages of being European. With steamships making travel easier, more Europeans were settling in Singapore; and the social schism between Europeans and Asians grew wider with Europeans taking refuge in their exclusionary social organizations that complemented the insurmountable barriers against advancement in the professional sphere. Racism was pervasive and contributed to the distinctive communal identities that were already taking shape.

The conflict between European and Asian attitudes had an unintended consequence: They provided a common perspective for the different Asian communities. This also developed in part due to the English-medium schools, which the best students from each of the three Asian communities could attend. This gave this group of elites a common experience, in addition to a common language (English), which bound them together psychologically. It also created a class-based gap between the English-educated Asian elites from each of the communities, and those without wealth or education, but it formed an important sense of cohesion and a basis for a broader common identity—not just Chinese, Indian, or Malay but a beginning sense of being Singaporean that would be an important connection in years to come.

WHAT DID NOT HAPPEN: DEFENSES FOR SINGAPORE

Britain's sole interest in Singapore from the beginning of the colonial period was as an international trade center and a source of revenue. This never really wavered. When the Crown took over control of the

Straits Settlements in 1867, its primary concern was that the colony not cost the government money. For this reason, Britain relied largely on its command of the seas to provide protection for Singapore and other colonies. The British constructed Fort Canning, but military assessment made it clear that it would be nearly worthless in defending the port. There could be some shots fired when an attack fleet was coming toward Singapore, but once it was actually in the harbor, nothing could be done. Defenses were, at best, minimal.

Every so often, there would be a spark of concern about world events, and eyes would turn to Singapore as a possible center for British naval activities; but then the threat would pass, and attention would move elsewhere. This happened in the 1860s when the Admiralty's fleeting interest in Singapore helped pave the way in the negotiations over the shift to crown colony status. It happened again in the 1880s when there was concern about the French moving into Indochina, possible fighting with Russia over Afghanistan, and a greater Japanese naval prowess. The Colonial Office indicated a willingness to defend the port, but the merchants also wanted defense of the town. Three decades of arguing about costs ensued. While there was debate in the 1890s about building a big dockyard for the British Navy, concerns grew about protecting the waters closer to Great Britain, and resources shifted in that direction.

Singapore survived World War I without a single upset except for a 10-day mutiny in 1915 by the single regiment that was left in Singapore. The 5th Light Infantry was composed of Indian Muslims from Punjab. Already out of sorts with Britain being at war against Muslim Turkey, when they were ordered to ship out for Hong Kong (leaving Singapore with no military units), they mutinied out of fear that they would instead be sent to fight Turkey or something equally unappealing. A combination of local effort (police, Singapore Volunteers, and the like) and the efforts of nearby French, Russian, and Japanese allied naval crews put down the mutiny and restored order. Within Singapore, the lasting effect was resentment within the Indian community because all Indians in Singapore had to register with the government. In terms of defenses, it illustrated how dependant Singapore would be on allied assistance, but Britain continued to view Singapore as being first and foremost about trade.

The interwar years, however, finally yielded a shift in this outlook. In assessing global risks and military strategy, the British War Office reached some important conclusions. First, it concluded that the ongoing use of Hong Kong as the base for all British naval operations in East Asia was not viable. Hong Kong was too vulnerable to a land-based attack.

Singapore was determined to be a better location, and the Singapore Strategy was developed. The first draft of the Singapore Strategy called for an extensive naval base to be built in Singapore along with accompanying airfields. The naval station was to be large enough to function as a base for the full fleet, which risk assessments indicated would be needed to defend British interests in Asia against a full assault from the Japanese Imperial Navy.

Once again, however, defense plans were scaled back. The cost assessments weighed heavily against an extensive naval base in Singapore, and as fears increased that the next war would begin in Europe rather than Asia, the pressure to defend the British home front from potential aggression coming via the North Sea lessened the incentive to invest so heavily in naval defenses in Singapore. While the Singapore Strategy remained Britain's master plan for Asia, it was based on gross misjudgments about Singapore's vulnerabilities and was significantly scaled back from the first, more extensive draft of the Singapore Strategy. In a few short years, Britain's miscalculations would become brutally evident because, while Singapore was able to sit out World War I, it was not so fortunate in World War II.

Overall, these decades of crown colony status were ones of profound change in Singapore. Its population rose dramatically with increased immigration from China and India. Despite being subject to world market fluctuations, it grew in significance and wealth as a port with the greater demand for rubber and tin and its position as a valuable coaling station for the new steamship trade. It experienced ongoing social problems but slowly improved on many of them. Finally, Singaporean residents developed meaningful communal identities, both within their groups, and to a certain degree, as Singaporeans. All of these developments set important foundations for what would come in the future.

NOTES

1. Max E. Fletcher, "The Suez Canal and World Shipping, 1869–1914," *The Journal of Economic History* 18 (1958): 556–573.

2. Ibid.

3. Quoted in C. M. Turnbull, *A History of Singapore, 1819–1988,* 2nd ed. (New York, NY: Oxford University Press, 1989), 82.

4. Ibid., 90.

5. Ibid., 93.

6. Carl A. Trocki, *Singapore: Wealth, Power and the Culture of Control* (New York, NY: Routledge, 2006), 30.

7. W. G. Huff, "Boom-or-Bust Commodities and Industrialization in Pre-World War II Malaya," *The Journal of Economic History* 62 (2002): 1074–1115.

8. Trocki, *Singapore: Wealth, Power and the Culture of Control*, 35–37.

9. Ibid., 31.

10. Quoted in Turnbull, *A History of Singapore*, 92.

11. Ibid., 127.

12. Huff, "Boom-or-Bust Commodities and Industrialization in Pre-World War II Malaya," 1078.

13. Trocki, *Singapore: Wealth, Power and the Culture of Control*, 64.

14. Amarjit Kaur, "International Migration in Malaysia and Singapore Since the 1880s: State policies, migration trends, and governance of migration" (paper presented at the meeting of the Asian Studies Association of Australia, Wollongong, Australia, June 26, 2006).

15. Trocki, *Singapore: Wealth, Power and the Culture of Control*, 64.

16. Turnbull, *A History of Singapore*, 114.

17. Ibid., 86.

18. Trocki, *Singapore: Wealth, Power and the Culture of Control*, 64.

19. Turnbull, *A History of Singapore*, 133.

5

Fortress Singapore to Syonan-to: World War II

One of the major debates regarding World War II is whether Singapore had to fall. Although the British largely ignored the island as a major naval station until the 1930s, it then became the basis of the Empire's defense in Asia, protecting the gateways to India to the west and Australia and New Zealand to the south. Some historians put its defensive importance in the Empire as second only to Britain itself. Despite this central position, however, Singapore fell with dramatic speed just a few weeks after Japan began the offensive against it. Many poor decisions on the part of British military and political figures, from the top to the bottom of the command chain, combined with Japanese strategic brilliance, led to this defeat. The ensuing years of Japanese occupation were ones of great suffering for most of the population. For some, this was due to scarcities that often accompany war, but for many it was the result of deliberately inhumane tactics used by the Japanese. This was a tragic episode in Singapore's history that still lingers in the collective memory.

THE INTERWAR YEARS AND THE SINGAPORE STRATEGY

Following World War I, "the war to end all wars" as it was known, the British government looked toward international cooperation to prevent future war. The international community created the League of Nations so countries could talk about their disagreements, and a disarmament movement reduced available weaponry to lessen countries' chances of going to war. In this climate, the British cabinet made several key decisions. First, it adopted the Ten Year Policy, which stated that Britain would not be involved in a major war for 10 years. Second, it developed the Singapore Strategy for the protection of the eastern part of the Empire. The Singapore Strategy was based on the idea that Singapore would be an island fortress and the bulwark against aggression toward any British Commonwealth holdings in the Asia-Pacific region. The Strategy was drafted in three successively weaker and less costly versions. Highly developed fortifications were planned, including a massive naval base, accompanying airfields, and extensive gun and artillery placements. However, the implementation of the Strategy became bogged down and little progress was made throughout the 1920s, largely due to British political issues and a lack of urgency as Britain pursued international cooperation to avoid war. Britain allowed its previous alliance treaty with Japan to lapse, preferring the international approach over narrower alliances. For example, in 1922, Britain, the United States, France, and Japan agreed to a Naval Limitation Treaty to restrict the size of their navies and refrain from building new bases in the Pacific. Singapore, rather than Hong Kong, was an optimal choice for the premier British naval base in East Asia, because Hong Kong was too vulnerable and Singapore was outside of the restricted zone for naval base development. Despite these intentions, the British government funneled little money toward the construction of the defensive apparatus needed in Singapore.

However, early in the 1930s, Japan began to show its hand as an aggressively expansive power. In 1931 Japan invaded Manchuria; in 1932 it withdrew from the League of Nations; in 1935 it withdrew from the London Disarmament Conference; in 1936 it rescinded its participation in the Washington Naval Agreements (1921), which limited the armaments the US, Britain, and Japan could use in the Pacific; in 1936 Japan also made a pact with Germany against communism, and by extension, the Soviet Union; and in 1937 Japan invaded China. There was little doubt as to the trajectory of Japan's behavior, so the British ramped up construction in Singapore for a heavy military presence to deter Japan's possible aggression. The Singapore Strategy called for a strong naval and air force presence in Singapore to protect British interests with an array of guns pointed out to sea to prevent an attack on the island. The idea of an attack coming over land down the Malay Peninsula was long dismissed, because military analysts believed the tropical jungles and difficult terrain would make it too unappealing to an invasion force.

However, by the late 1930s, as construction progressed on the Sembawang Naval Base on the Johor Strait in the north of Singapore and on the associated military installations that extended to Changi on the east coast, Major-General Sir William Dobbie, General Officer Commanding for Malaya Command, issued a reassessment of the assumption that an invasion of Singapore would come by sea. Dobbie concluded that the commanders in London had not taken into account the more extensive road and railroad networks that had been developed down the Malay Peninsula, which provided pathways through jungle and around difficult terrain for invaders. He also questioned the ongoing assumption that the Japanese would avoid any invasion during the monsoon season, which caused high waves and wind. Indeed, the discovery that 5,000 Chinese laborers had been smuggled into the Malay States in the middle of the monsoon season was an evidentiary blow to that assumption.[1] In fact, the monsoon-associated cloud cover would help hide an invading force, making a monsoon invasion more attractive. Planners also assumed that Japan would not be able to access airfields that were close enough to offer air support for an invasion, and that superior British intelligence would provide ample warning of a pending invasion. Finally, they believed reinforcements in the form of Britain's main fleet could be brought to Singapore's aid in a mere 42 days, should an invasion actually be mounted.

In response to Dobbie's new risk assessment, military officials revised the plan, calling it *Operation Matador*. They concluded that an attack via the Malay Peninsula would likely come from far in the north around the Thai border and that the Royal Air Force (RAF) would need to launch air assaults, while the Royal Naval launched assaults on landing forces, before the invaders could become established and move down the Malay Peninsula. In preparation, the military constructed a series of small airbases far in the north of the Peninsula. *Matador* was the crucial addendum to the Singapore Strategy that was supposed to maintain its viability for defending the Empire in the Asia-Pacific.

However, there remained a problematic disconnect between plan and implementation. Despite the whole strategy hinging on deterrence through naval and air power, the British government became increasingly reluctant to direct resources where they may never be needed, particularly as the political situation in Europe worsened. At a 1937 Imperial Conference on strategies for the protection of the British Commonwealth, there was a discussion about whether waiting until the threat was at hand to send out ships would be adequate defense. The Australians, in particular, doubted Britain's ability to send enough ships when a war was already going on and the Chiefs of Staff (the top military leadership in London) suggested that a naval base without ships was not much of a deterrent. Still, the government balked at drawing naval resources away from Europe.

In 1938, the King George VI Dry Dock opened at the Sembawang Naval Base to much acclaim. The anti-aircraft and artillery defenses were also in place and Singapore had some of the best defenses in the world. There was much rhetoric about the impregnable "Fortress Singapore." Unfortunately, while the installations were in place, the shipyard remained empty, as did the air bases, both on Singapore and in northern Malaysia. The rhetoric of Fortress Singapore did not match the reality.

In the ensuing months, the international situation grew worse. The war in Europe that started in September 1939 commanded Britain's full attention and resources. Singapore and the Malay States were Britain's "dollar arsenal" and their contribution to the war effort was to keep the funds and the commodities flowing. At the start of the World War II, the Malay Peninsula was the source of 40 percent of the world's rubber and 60 percent of the world's tin, most of which was sold to the United States. Singapore ranked second in revenue within the Commonwealth, just behind Canada.[2] In the early months in the European war, all did not go well and by June 1940, Britain was forced to reassess its defensive posture. Italy had joined the effort on Germany's side, and France and the Netherlands had collapsed. Britain would have to rely on the U.S. naval fleet in Hawaii to deter the Japanese, despite the United States having signaled that it would not go out of its way to save the various British, French, and Dutch territories in Asia. In June, Germany attacked the Soviet Union, which freed the Japanese from the possibility of Soviet attack, allowing them to devote their full attention toward advancing their goals elsewhere.

In July, the United States placed economic sanctions on Japan that severely threatened their war effort in China. The Japanese determined that they had a choice: They could give up their war on China or they could secure their own supply of war materials. Japan's economic interests in Southeast Asia were already considerable. As early as 1922, when the idea of building the Sembawang Naval Base on the Johor Strait was presented to Sultan Ibrahim of Johor, he noted that Japan leased 30,000 acres of state-owned land for rubber plantation in Johor, which was in close proximity to the proposed naval base. The British disregarded the warning.[3] Moreover, throughout the 1920s and 1930s, Japan also made extensive investments in the tin mines of the Malay Peninsula. A 1939 report on agricultural interests in the Malay Peninsula expressed concern about Japan's extensive interests in the region, noting that in 1935, Japan accounted for 7 percent of imports and 12 percent of exports of Singapore, and that, "The mercantile population of Singapore fear that the Japanese will soon dominate the shipping and banking interests of the colony."[4] With the added factor of economic sanctions from the United States, the Japanese chose to secure their war materials, which made the Malay Peninsula and the Dutch East Indies (today Indonesia) of great value. Japan signed a treaty of alliance with Germany and Italy; and through Germany's connection with the Nazi-affiliated Vichy government in France, Japan gained access to French airbases in Indochina (today Vietnam, Cambodia, and Laos). These airbases put them within much closer striking distance of the Malay Peninsula.

Japan began making plans for an assault on the Malay Peninsula and Singapore in fall 1940, but it was July 1941 when leaders made the final decision to go forward. The Japanese, like the British, determined that the best approach was to invade far in the north, even into Thailand, then move to the western side of the Peninsula where the road network was better, and then proceed to Singapore. The plan hinged on a surprise attack that was a speedy and efficient sweep to overwhelm British and Commonwealth forces before they could mount an effective defense. Knowing that British defensive efforts were lacking for air and sea warfare, the Japanese calculated that it would be a contest of speed to see if the Japanese Imperial Army could take Singapore first or if reinforcements would arrive first and beat them back. The goal was to take Singapore in fewer than 100 days. If they deprived the Anglo-American alliance of their base in the area, then they could divide and conquer, taking the resources they needed from Indonesia, the Philippines, Malaysia, and Burma to finish the war with China. Lieutenant-Colonel Masanobi Tsuji was put in charge of planning and training, and the actual operation was put under the command of one of Japan's most esteemed generals, Lieutenant-General Tomoyuki Yamashita. Shortly before the invasion, Yamashita was confident; Germany had managed to intercept Britain's readiness assessment for the Far East, which made it clear how ill-prepared they were for a war in the East and how low on the priority list it was compared to the European theater. Germany passed the document to Japan, giving Yamashita clear evidence of what he and his troops were facing.

Meanwhile, the British were still focused on Singapore and Malaysia being their dollar arsenal and continued to debate their defense strategy should the Japanese attack. The local commanders had repeatedly asked for ships, planes, and soldiers. They received very few planes; in fact, some that could have gone to Singapore were given to the Soviet Union to help its war effort. Troops were sent primarily from India and Australia. Decision-makers in London decided in August of 1940 that the naval base had to be protected at all costs and that the RAF would have to do it by protecting the Malay Peninsula. There was considerable disagreement about whether that defense should occur to the north, where there were the scattered airbases, or whether a more focused defense in Johor should be attempted instead. Unfortunately, the RAF planes could not be sent until the end of 1941 because the British military was overextended. In January 1941, British Prime Minister Winston Churchill decided that since Singapore was such a well-defended fortress, RAF reinforcements were not necessary and a waste of resources that could be used elsewhere. He concluded that the Japanese would not attack such a well-protected fortress unless things were going terribly for the British in Europe. In any case, the United States would respond. In debate after debate, civilian and military decision makers in London concluded that they had time to send needed equipment later and that the Japanese would not attack. The Joint Intelligence Committee determined in spring of 1941 that the Soviet Union would more likely be Japan's first target. In late September, a meeting of local military officials in Singapore informed London that Japan would not attack any time soon, and certainly not before the end of the monsoon season in February, despite intercepted Japanese intelligence suggesting otherwise, and Japan's activities in the French holdings of Indochina. Despite his confidence in Fortress Singapore and the certainty that Japan would not attack soon, Churchill decided to send a few ships to Singapore. It was certainly not the main fleet that the Singapore Strategy called for, nor was it a substantial secondary fleet supported by the Chiefs of Staff in London. Instead, it was a minifleet, known as Force Z, of what could be spared from the more critical war efforts closer to home. The most notable of the ships was the brand new HMS *Prince of Wales* that was the pride of the British navy and nicknamed the "HMS Unsinkable." This battleship was accompanied by a cruiser and a handful of smaller ships, of which half were in disrepair. An aircraft carrier was dispatched, but it ran aground and never arrived. Thus, Force Z was essentially too small to do any good as a deterrent and too compromised to function as a fighting fleet without the protection of air support. Decision-making in London was fraught with disagreements and poor communication between civilian and military commanders (exacerbated by grossly erroneous underestimations of Japan's intentions and overestimations of Singapore's defenses) and ultimately overwhelmed by the war closer to home. A possible war in faraway Asia was far outweighed by the war already at Britain's door.

The situation on the ground in Singapore was no better. Military officials from the different branches and command centers disagreed on strategy and lacked a centralized command structure to override their differences. They, like officials in London, did not believe Japan would attack in the near future. In the interest of keeping up appearances, they made no efforts at civilian defense. Both military and civilian leaders feared that if they focused too much on building further ground defense installations or initiated programs incorporating civilians into defense, it would weaken the faith of the people in Britain's strength, cause an unwelcome panic, and potentially undermine Britain's hold over the colony. Thus, in sharp contrast to Britain where civil defense programs were extensive, in Singapore virtually nothing was done. This was shocking to the Chief Engineer of Malaya Command, Ivan Simson, when he arrived in Singapore in August 1941 from London, where civilian defense program planning and implementation was in full force. He promptly developed a plan for improved local defenses that would have placed anti-tank and gun provisions on main roads, mines on bridges, special defenses in Johor, and defense works on the north shore of Singapore. The general in charge of the army in Singapore-based Malaya Command, Lieutenant-General Arthur Percival, received the recommendations but did not implement the plan.

On December 1, 1941 a state of emergency was declared. Percival indicated concern but was not overly worried. Nevertheless, there was a great deal of excitement when, on December 2, Force Z, without the aircraft carrier, sailed up the Johor Strait toward the naval base. The admiral in charge was so alarmed by its vulnerability without any air cover that he suggested taking the ships immediately to the Philippines, but they remained in Singapore. On December 3, Percival made a statement over the radio that an attack was not likely and that, while he was hoping more aircraft would arrive, what they had on hand would be adequate if anything did occur.

THE JAPANESE ATTACK

The Japanese strategy to obtain the resources of Southeast Asia risked war with both the United States and Great Britain. Since speed and surprise were central to the plan, they opted for a first strike. On December 8, 1941 (in the Tokyo time zone), Japan launched a sea-based attack on Kota Bahru on the northern part of the Malay Peninsula at 1:40 a.m.; Japanese forces landed at Singora and Patani in southern Thailand at 3:05 a.m.; they bombed Pearl Harbor, Hawaii, at 3:20 a.m. and bombed Singapore's Seletar and Tangah airbases and Raffles Place in the city center at 6:10 a.m. At 11:40 a.m. Emperor Hirohito issued an Imperial Order declaring war on the United States and Great Britain.[5] Japan also quickly launched attacks against Hong Kong and the Philippines.

The local commanders in Singapore were paralyzed by indecision. Sir Robert Brooke-Popham, Commander-in-Chief of the Far East (of land and air forces but not naval or civilian), had received authorization from London on December 5 to commence with *Operation Matador* when he believed an invasion was pending. *Matador*, the whole basis for the defense of Singapore in case of an assault from the north, could only succeed if it were implemented quickly and decisively. It was essential that British and Commonwealth forces reach the likely landing points in Thailand before the Japanese landed and stop the invader's advance at several other critical junctures. For example, an area known as The Ledge, a narrow road cut in a cliffside on a main thoroughfare leading south from Thailand, could be blown up to block an advancing army. Likewise, the various airbases in northern Malaysia (that never had adequate numbers of aircraft to help with defense) had to be protected lest they fall into enemy hands and become support for Japanese operations. The thinly scattered troops around the bases in the north would not be able to hold the bases against the full onslaught of an advancing army, which underscored the urgency of stopping the invasion immediately. On December 6, Japanese naval convoys were spotted, but their destination was not yet certain. Thailand was officially neutral, so invading prematurely could have started a conflict, thus Brooke-Popham held off on launching *Matador* until it was confirmed that the ships were heading for the Malay Peninsula. He did not receive that confirmation until the night of December 7, and by then it was too late to send defending forces to the predicted (with total accuracy) landing sites. *Operation Matador* was abandoned immediately with no ready back-up plan. The other aspect of the Singapore Strategy, the prompt deployment of reinforcements of naval and air power and human backup, also came to naught. Initially, it was expected that help could arrive in six weeks, although it was revised upwards several times through the years. By 1941, it was calculated that Singapore would have to hold out for six months on its own before help would arrive. That was far too long.

Admiral Tom Phillips set out to sea quickly after the attack began, partly so that his small fleet would not be easy targets for Japanese bombing runs, and partly with the hope of intercepting further landings of Japanese troops on the Malay Peninsula. He departed before learning that the airfield at Kota Bahru was already in Japanese hands. Thus, without his own aircraft carrier, he would not have any air support to protect the ships from above. He attempted to turn back the fleet since the mission was too risky without any air cover; but on December 10, Japanese bombers found them; and within hours the ships were sunk, even the HMS Unsinkable. This was a devastating loss for the British and a boon to morale for the Japanese. Inside two days, the Japanese controlled the seas, and soon the air. Within 24 hours, Japan destroyed more than half of the few planes in the northern parts of the Malay Peninsula and held the inadequately defended airfields. The days that followed revealed a recurrent pattern of poor decisions that did nothing to stop the Japanese drive southward. Heavy reliance on ground forces was never part of the plan to defend Singapore, and Percival refused to take risks that could have potentially altered the outcome. His orders were to protect the Sembawang Naval Base at all costs. To do that, he tried to follow the general strategy developed as part of *Operation Matador* and keep the fighting as far away from Singapore as possible. Percival continued to do what he did before the start of the attack: He scattered ground troops around the northern part of Malaysia to defend many different fixed positions (such as airfields and roads) that were valuable to the Japanese war effort, but the troops were dispersed too thinly to mount a successful defense at any of the points of engagement. Worse, with the Japanese controlling air and sea and being highly mobile on the ground, Yamashita was able to move around the fixed Allied positions, threatening to cut them off from behind. Yamashita had considerable resources at hand at the start of the invasion: naval support, more than 200 tanks, 80,000 combat troops, and about 600 aircraft for the campaign.[6] British and Commonwealth troops lacked effective anti-tank weapons and some fighters had barely even seen a tank; their sole advantage was in number of soldiers. Percival's orders to them were consistent but contradictory: troops were to give their all to defend their position but not lose so many fighters as to become overly weakened as fighting units. By trying to defend so many different points, Percival was giving Yamashita a divide and conquer advantage. It was still a race between the Japanese advance and the arrival of reinforcements, so the defending troops had to retain enough strength to hold on until help could arrive for what Percival considered the main battle.

There continued to be destructive disagreement between local military leaders. Concerned that Percival's tactic of spreading out the troops left them too dispersed to turn the tide, other commanders argued that troops should be pulled back and concentrated at a point farther south on the Peninsula, even as far as Johor, to make a unified stand. En route, the retreating army could blow up bridges and destroy roads to slow the Japanese advance. This would also have the advantage of lengthening the Japanese supply lines while shortening the Allied supply lines. This debate went on for weeks, with Percival resisting and continuing to try to keep the fighting as far away as possible, as it relentlessly moved closer. The Japanese advance was swift: they took Penang by December 17, Taiping by December 22, crossed the Slim River by January 7, took Kuala Lumpur by January 11, crossed the Muar River just south of Melaka on January 15, and pushed onward into Johor.

In mid-December 1941, Churchill's reaction was that Singapore needed to hold strong while Britain and the United States developed a coordinated strategy for the war in the Pacific, and he set sail for Washington, D.C. to do that. When reinforcement troops arrived, Percival sent them into action; but due to heavy losses, reinforcements were merely replacements rather than a strengthening of forces that could halt the Japanese advance. Churchill recommended retreat to a defensive line in Johor to protect the island fortress of Singapore, still not understanding that there were no defensive works in Johor to form a line around or that Singapore was in no way a fortress. Percival, with the approval of the Chiefs of Staff, instead opted to continue his strategy of trying to keep the fighting farther north. By Christmas, the Chiefs of Staff felt the urgency of the situation; and a joint American-British-Dutch-Australian Command was developed under General Archibald Wavell, the Commander-in-Chief of India. However, they could still not react quickly enough to the pace of events. The loss of an airbase in Burma meant that fighter aircraft from India could not be flown in; all reinforcements, both people and equipment, would have to come by sea.

By mid-January 1942, with the Japanese Imperial Army having advanced past Kuala Lumpur, there was no choice but to retreat to

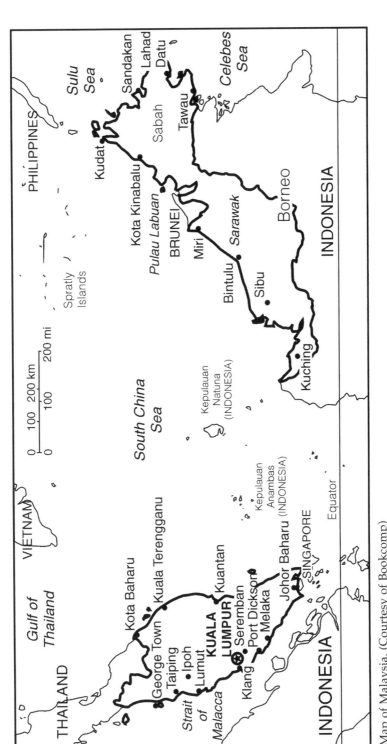

Map of Malaysia. (Courtesy of Bookcomp)

Johor. Churchill finally grasped the nature of Singapore's problematic defenses, constructed with the expectation of a sea invasion, and that Singapore was in no respect a fortress. He wrote a scathing memo to the Chiefs of Staff,

> Seaward batteries and a naval base do not constitute a fortress, which is a *completely encircled* strong place. Merely to have seaward batteries and no forts or fixed defences to protect their rear is not to be excused on any ground. By such neglect the whole security of the fortress has been placed at the mercy of ten thousand men breaking across the straits in small boats. I warn you this will be one of the greatest possible scandals that could possibly be exposed.[7]

Churchill was nevertheless shocked when he was told just a few days later, on January 21, that Singapore would not hold for long after Johor fell, as it did on January 27. Ongoing communication problems and tactical disagreements between Churchill and the military chiefs, and a large set of false assumptions on Churchill's behalf led to a devastating lack of coordination.

THE FALL OF SINGAPORE

In Singapore the situation was rapidly deteriorating. Japanese bombing raids had resumed at the end of December and intensified from the middle of January onward with a frequency of up to a half a dozen each day. In the densely constructed living spaces of Singapore, especially in Chinese areas, the casualty rates were immense with estimates of at least 10,000 people killed and many more injured.[8] Despite the obviously worsening situation, government censors prohibited media reports about how poorly the defense of the Malay Peninsula was progressing. The administration still feared loss of confidence in colonial authority, or worse, mass panic, and made no provisions, such as air raid shelters, to protect the population. Finally on February 7, local officials invited the population to participate in civilian defenses, if they wished but did not convey a sense of urgency. Overall, civilian leadership was weak. The population was willing to help and many volunteers came forward, but the organization or coordination needed to create last-minute civilian defenses was absent. The one exception was the creation of Dalforce, a group of Singaporean Chinese who volunteered to be guerilla fighters. This materialized too late and in the end Dalforce was sent out but with limited weapons and almost no ammunition.

Military leaders prepared for a last stand in Singapore. Troops retreated from the Peninsula and a 60-yard-wide hole was blasted in the causeway that connected Singapore with Johor. Unfortunately, piping on the causeway carried a portion of Singapore's water supply from Johor, which made the water supply potentially scarce, should a siege develop. The meager defensive preparation in Singapore shocked the retreating troops. There had been discussions of creating defensive installations and some were even marked on maps, but there were fears that suddenly having to erect defenses would be harmful to morale, so leaders left it until the last hour when there was no other choice. Soldiers set to work assembling defensive works, but time was short. More reinforcements came in, but the losses in the preceding weeks were great enough that the reinforcements were, again, replacements rather than added strength. To make matters worse, they were mostly barely trained, new recruits.

Miscalculations still plagued Percival. He assumed the Japanese forces were much larger than they actually were and that they would attack from many different positions. He figured there initially would be a large, concentrated assault on a specific target in Singapore, with additional invasion waves behind it. Thus, following a similar troop dispersal strategy as he had used on the Peninsula, he stationed troops along the coastline around the island rather than concentrating them on the exposed and largely defenseless north shore or in a strategic location like Bukit Timah, the highest point in Singapore (538 feet), and the site of water reservoirs and supply depots. Moreover, the plan was improvised, because the still-disagreeing military leadership in Singapore had not developed a plan while they still had time. Singapore had impressive gun fortifications, but they were designed to defend against a marine invasion, not an invasion from the north. The guns could have been turned, but even then, they were designed to shoot at ships, not at tanks or people, and proved useless in the final defense of the island.

On the Japanese side, Yamashita was concerned about his supply lines. He knew he lacked adequate reserves to stage a protracted siege of Singapore, thus speed remained a strategic priority for him. Once Johor fell, he opted for an invasion across the narrowest part of the Johor Strait on the northwest side of Singapore, just west of the causeway. He had 300 collapsible boats, which, if connected together, could transport not only his soldiers but also artillery, and he had full command of the air. He commenced his invasion of Singapore on

February 8, 1942. Yamashita knew the Johor Strait had not been mined, so Japanese forces were able to slip across under the cover of darkness and up creeks and inlets. Australian soldiers stationed on that part of the island were surrounded quickly.

What ensued was a military disaster. Phone and radio communications buckled, leading to confusion. While the military commanders of the mostly British, Indian, and Australian units had the improvised plan, a number of them did not follow it and left gaps in an already weak defense. Percival, falsely certain that Yamashita had many more troops, continued to keep Allied forces scattered along the coast waiting for the secondary invasion that never came. Troops were given a conflicting mission: they were supposed to defend the island (Churchill was still insisting that Singapore could not fall), while at the same time destroying anything that might be of use to the Japanese–oil and rubber supplies, a tin smelting factory, and the naval base that had been the defend-at-all-costs focus of Percival's orders from London.

The final Japanese assault began on February 11. Military and civilian leadership were still in disarray and indecisive. While some Allied troops put up a strong fight, others did not. Some government leaders and police walked off the job. Civilians simply tried to survive. Some tried to flee to the port and escape in boats. Japanese planes shot them on the piers; and most of those who made it onto boats were caught, and some were killed. In the city center, at least a million people within a three-mile radius of the port suffered the bombing raids. Estimates range as high as 2,000 civilian fatalities per day in the last days of the fighting.[9] The Japanese, their supplies running ever lower, pushed for speed. By February 14, they had repaired the hole in the causeway and were able to bring in heavier guns and tanks, hoping to finish the fight quickly. As illustration of just how bad the defense was, Australian troops found a map showing Japanese plans for February 14 but were told to conserve ammunition since supplies were so low. Even as they received confirmation that the Japanese were moving ahead with the plan on the map, Australian soldiers under the command of Major-General H. Gordon Bennett could see the Japanese advancing and did not shoot. Yamashita was also running low on ammunition, so low that afterwards he and the strategist Tsuji estimated that had fighting gone on for just three more days, they would have been forced to end their attack. However, instead of conserving, he ordered his troops to bluff by firing heavily and leading British commanders to think they had unlimited supplies. On the morning of February 15, Percival met with military leaders at Fort Canning.

They were low on ammunition, fuel, food, and were concerned about the water supply. The conditions were grim, and they had no idea of Yamashita's true situation. If they continued to fight, combat would move into the city center, which would be devastating to civilians; they felt that continuing was futile. While they were meeting, a telegram arrived authorizing Percival to surrender. At 5:30 p.m. that afternoon, Percival went to the Japanese Headquarters carrying a white flag for the largest surrender of troops in British history. It happened in just 70 days, 30 days faster than the Japanese had hoped, and nearly four months before the estimated six months it would have taken the British to bring in adequate reinforcements in the 1941 assessment for the Singapore Strategy. In the race between the Japanese advances versus the arrival of British reinforcements, the Japanese were swifter by far.

HOW DID IT GO WRONG?

Much has been written about why the fight for Singapore was such a disaster for the British. Clearly there were many facets to the failure, both from top levels of civilian and military command in London down to local commanders and troops on the ground. The disaster was not one of short-term making: Many scholars point to the Singapore Strategy as flawed from its inception in the early 1920s, seeing it as something between a gamble and a bluff.

In terms of poor decisions at the highest levels, many critics point to Churchill and the top military leadership who failed to make a realistic and coherent plan once Japan's aggression and Singapore's vulnerabilities had been revealed in the mid-1930s. The physical defenses were inadequate and under-resourced; empty naval bases and airfields do not project impressive deterrent power. Squabbling among civilian and military leaders in the years leading up to the war and after it began hindered planning. Rather than hashing out their differences until a conclusion was reached, matters were dropped and ignored until it was too late. This led, in part, to some of Churchill's lack of understanding about Singapore's defenses. Funding choices are also a target of criticism. The British government hoped to defend its Asian colonies at minimal cost and was not willing to invest funds in an Eastern Fleet that may have been a genuine deterrent to Japan and, at the very least, could have tipped the scales in favor of Britain. Some scholars argue that all through the 1920s and 1930s, Britain should have been building more ships and aircraft so the resources would have been available when needed. Finally, the choices made about the available resources were poor and sometimes based on political considerations rather than strategic necessity. Some would say that delaying air, naval, and human resources in 1941 was a wrong choice; however, the situation was one of competing demands and the war in Europe, closest to the British home front, received the highest priority. However, it appears to have been very much a political decision over a strategic one when the Soviet Union received aircraft that could have been sent to Singapore, with probably much greater impact than they made added to existing Soviet air power.

In terms of failures at the local level, specific criticisms have been levied against the commanders on the ground and Percival in particular. The decisions, both on the Malay Peninsula and in the Battle of Singapore, to disperse troops to a point where they were too scattered to be effective rather than risk a concentrated stand, was perhaps the poorest strategy. The hesitations in decision-making, such as the delayed implementation of *Operation Matador*, were also problematic. Some of those poor decisions may have been caused by the fragmented command structure that put no one in the region in control of all aspects of the war effort. The fragmentation almost certainly led to various arguments over strategy and other conflicts among commanders on the ground, to the point of some not following orders at the end. Australian troops have received blame, particularly for their actions at the very end of the battle when they did not fight. The criticisms have been sharp enough that it has become a politically sensitive topic and the Australian government has noted the very significant fight the Australians put up along the Malay Peninsula. Another local failing was the lack of involvement of the civilian population. Had civilians been organized to help with defenses or conscripted to fight as part of the army, perhaps the outcome could have been different. Instead, beyond losing the labor contributions the civilians could have made, the local military and civilian administrations left the civilian population vulnerable simply to hide how poorly the fight was going and to avoid appearing weak. Despite the dense urban dwellings, no air raid shelters were built that could have saved some of the thousands of lives lost in the bombings.

Overarching many of these upper- and lower-level problems in decision-making are an array of false perceptions that harmed the overall effort. Churchill appeared to have believed the myth that Singapore was a genuine fortress, with battlements all around and a moat comprised of the Johor Strait. His concern was how long Singapore could hold out under a siege, not whether Singapore could last long enough for a siege to begin. Churchill also thought the United States would make an effort to save Singapore and indeed expressed relief that Pearl Harbor was bombed simultaneously, assuring the U.S. entry into the war, believing that Singapore would then be saved. Poor intelligence was also a contributing factor, because the British did not have the information they needed and their perceptions were such that they had no idea how poor the intelligence gathered actually was. Thus they did not receive detailed warnings prior to the invasion. Another explanation that has been offered is racism: the British simply could not believe that Japanese/non-Whites could develop a sophisticated strategy with good technology that could completely overwhelm the British Empire, even though they had evidence before them. If they saw the Japanese doing something differently than was the norm in the British military, they assumed it would be an inferior approach, rather than one suited to local conditions.

Finally, imperial overstretch is a common explanation of the British failure. The Empire was simply too large for its available resources to defend. When Britain had to channel so many of its resources to the war in Europe as well as Africa and the Middle East, there was little that could be spared for the relatively late arrival to the war, Southeast Asia. The British Empire spanned too much territory to protect. All that said, and with most explanations clearly focused on British failings, one must not forget the effective strategy and implementation by the Japanese. The Imperial Japanese Army was a strong fighting force that struck hard and fast and pushed past anything the British put in its path. The Japanese strategists accurately assessed the strengths and weaknesses of the opponent prior to attack and the resulting plan was carried out with precision.

While there is no shortage of what-ifs and if-onlys, the reality is that Britain's failure to defend Singapore was multifaceted. Of course more money could have been spent or funds could have been allocated differently. Decision-making in London and in Singapore could have been different, from the 1920s through the end of the fight. In the end, however, it is important to look at outcomes. The control of the Malay Peninsula allowed the Japanese to conquer significant portions of Indonesia, which together with Malaysia, offered resources such as oil and rubber, which were vital to the Japanese war effort. As a port, Singapore proved unimportant to the Japanese; because world trade, the constant source of revenue for Singapore, was too disrupted to yield much income. Militarily, the port was not needed. Australia and New Zealand were invested in the security of Singapore because they saw it as a bulwark against aggression toward them, but Japan never launched an invasion against either country, so this threat did not materialize. However, while the loss of Singapore may not have proved ultimately disastrous to the overall Allied war effort, it was unquestionably a blow to morale. There were debates about strategy and reinforcements in 1941 and 1942 before Singapore was even lost, and one member of the British Parliament labeled it "the Worst Disaster since Ethelred the Unready,"[10] a reference to the English king who lost most of the country's territory to Viking invaders in the late 900s.

THE OCCUPATION

Japanese forces formally occupied the island on February 16, 1942. People, anxious about what would happen, stayed home rather than opening shops and businesses. They had even made an effort in the last days before the capitulation to dump supplies of liquor so that drunkenness would not add to the feared rampage of rape, murder, and destruction that often follows military conquest. As it was, the takeover was orderly with the military police establishing control in the city center and the army being held back, although there were some instances of conquest violence in the northwest portion of Singapore.

Treatment of Prisoners of War and Civilian Internees

Japanese authorities immediately took an approach of treating the various ethnic groups differently, which over the years of the occupation reinforced the differences between them. European and British Commonwealth citizens, both soldiers and civilians, were imprisoned. The soldiers, approximately 50,000 in all, were treated as prisoners of war (POWs) and held in barracks at Changi on the southeast part of Singapore.[11] Civilians, about 2,000 initially, although the number eventually grew to 3,500, were interred in Changi Jail.[12] Indian troops (about 45,000) and the few Malay soldiers (about 600) were ordered to appear at Farrer Park on February 17 at which time they were encouraged to switch their loyalties to Emperor Hirohito. The Japanese were clearly anticipating enthusiasm from the local communities for their liberation from colonial control. However, the way the Japanese handled many aspects of the occupation made gratitude impossible. The Indian troops were invited to fight against British colonialism in India with the Indian National Army. With few exceptions, the professional soldiers among the Indians refused to switch loyalties, and some were tortured and killed. About 20,000 of them agreed to join the Indian National Army, but for most that was likely an opportunistic decision to avoid harsh treatment from the Japanese. The rest were treated as POWs. Among the Malays, the officers who refused to switch sides were executed, and then their troops were told they could return home. However, the first hundred or so who were supposedly being given a ride to the train station were executed.[13] The rest returned to their families, many of whom had followed their family members to Singapore during the Japanese advance down the Peninsula. In terms of dealing with the enemy soldiers and swaying them to their cause, the Japanese efforts were not successful.

For most of the POWs and the civilian internees, the experience was mixed. Both groups were able to eke out a fairly comfortable existence in many respects. The POWs had an active social life in the camps with swimming and theatrical entertainments performed by the prisoners. They even made "Changi University" where as many as 2,000 POW students participated in classes offered by fellow prisoners with lectures on topics ranging from physics to law to languages. Among the internees, they formed a democratically elected government within the jail to have representative liaisons with prison officials. They played bridge, had musical events, and even started their own jail newspapers, such as the *Changi Guardian*. Food rations for both groups were not extensive, but they were consistent throughout the war until the very end when food became scarce and some civilian and military prisoners suffered malnutrition and starvation.

On the downside, both groups were forced into work units, a violation of international standards for the treatment of prisoners in wartime, which dictate that prisoners should not be required to assist with the enemy's war effort. In Singapore, prisoners tried to strike a balance between working hard enough to avoid being beaten and slowly enough to minimize help to the Japanese. Officials forced prisoners to rebuild the port and roads and, as one of their more noteworthy projects, built the airfield that was the foundation for today's Changi International Airport, Singapore's main airport. The worst labor assignment was for those shipped north to work on the Burma-Thailand Railway from October 1942 to October 1943. Sixty thousand prisoners, working under terrible conditions, built the 260-mile rail line at the cost of about 15,000 prisoner lives.[14]

The worst incident for civilian internees happened as a result of what is known as the Double Tenth Event. In October 1943, a small group of Allied special forces rowed canoes into the harbor during the night on a sabotage mission known as *Operation Jaywick*, and managed to destroy seven ships, including an oil tanker. Japanese authorities could not believe this had been carried out without assistance from people in Singapore and concluded that the internees were the most likely culprits. They were assembled in Changi Jail while their

possessions were searched and then dozens were taken away for interrogation and torture by military police. No connection to the sabotage
was found and the Japanese finally discovered what had happened a
little over a year later when another special forces unit was captured
while attempting another raid. Conditions in Changi Jail deteriorated
for the internees after the Double Tenth Event. Eventually the internees were moved to a different location, where the situation grew even
worse for some of them, especially women who were forced into sexual slavery as "comfort women" for Japanese soldiers.

Treatment of the Civilian Population

The civilian population, now swollen to 1.4 million people by an
influx of refugees from the Malay Peninsula, also suffered greatly.
The Japanese generally treated the Indians and Malays more kindly
than the 700,000 Singaporean Chinese,[15] who were not trusted by the
Japanese because of Singaporean Chinese support for the war effort
against the Japanese in China and perhaps a general bias against
Chinese people after five years of war. The Japanese planned to make
Singapore a permanent colony, so they knew they needed to win over
the Chinese population. They first had to purge the Chinese community of any untrustworthy elements, so they launched a brief but
brutal program called *sook ching* or "purging for purification." On
February 18, officials ordered all Chinese males between the ages of
18 and 50 to report to evaluation centers. The *Kempeitai* or military
police were in charge and were highly trained in interrogation.
Auxiliaries with less training were also pulled in from the regular
army. Some of the interrogations were systematic and quick; others
were arbitrary and lasted for days during which people were without
food, water, and shelter. The military police also used informers from
the local population who, while wearing hoods to conceal their identities, helped the Japanese look for suspicious characters. The simplest
criteria were adequate to raise suspicion and could include certain
professions, for example teachers or journalists, which were two
professions to which recent immigrants from China had tended to
gravitate; in other cases a tattoo might be enough to raise the suspicion
of authorities, because that could be an indicator of secret society membership. At some of the evaluation centers all members of the Hainanese
community were suspect, because the Hainan region in China was
notorious for its support of the Chinese communist movement. Other
targets were supporters of the *Guomindang* movement in China. For
some people, writing their name in the Roman alphabet rather than in

Chinese or having worked for Europeans was suspicious. Anyone suspected of being in Dalforce was a target. Overall, decisions were quite indiscriminate and inconsistent. Once the sorting was complete, those who were cleared were marked with a symbol and released; those not cleared were otherwise marked, and although some were imprisoned, most were soon executed. They were taken out to sea, tied together and dumped overboard, or taken to the beach, herded out into the sea and shot to death. It is not known how many ethnic Chinese were exterminated in what some scholars (e.g., Murfett et al.) called ethnic cleansing, but estimates are as high as 50,000 or more.[16]

The *sook ching* was one of several policies implemented in the early days that convinced many people (especially the Chinese community) that avoiding the attention of the authorities was a wise choice for survival. In an attempt to ensure public order and prevent looting, Japanese soldiers sometimes fired into crowds. If individual looters were caught, they may be let free with a warning if they were Indian or Malay, but if they were Chinese, they were often executed and their heads put on public display as a lesson to others. The gruesome evidence of how far the Japanese military went to assure order was perhaps part of the reason no real opposition movement developed in Singapore during the occupation. Even though the *sook ching* only lasted the first week or so, the military police continued to be a source of enormous fear and intimidation throughout the occupation. If citizens were suspected of opposing the occupation, or made a negative comment about a government action, or complained about food shortages, or were found to have western ties (such as books or music or being English-educated), they could be arrested and interrogated. The interrogations typically involved torture, and many died in custody. With time, the threat of informing on someone to the military police also became a method of settling vendettas and of blackmailing people, because actual guilt or innocence was irrelevant and only one informant was needed to merit arrest. Typically, the only escape from military police custody was bribery. Moreover, being cleared by one military police office did not mean a person was cleared by all; a person could potentially be arrested by a different office and have to repeat the entire process. This sort of treatment made it difficult for the Japanese to evoke positive sentiments from many in the population. Japanese officials made some attempts at benevolent rule, such as mostly leaving people alone in their religious practices and opening a couple of amusement parks, but the attempts did not counter the widespread climate of fear.

A special economic targeting was also enacted toward the Chinese population. As evidence of their loyalty and to raise revenue for the war effort, the administration demanded a "gift" of $50 million from the Chinese population in the Malay States and Singapore, with Singapore's portion set at $10 million. This amount was approximately a quarter of the currency in circulation,[17] so it was an enormous sum of money to collect, and they only had a matter of weeks to do so. In Singapore, any Chinese citizens with property valued at over $3,000 were required to pay an 8 percent tax toward the gift and businesses had to pay a 5 percent tax on their holdings. The full sum was not collected in time, even with a short extension on the deadline, and so they had to arrange for a loan from a Japanese bank to cover nearly half the amount due, with repayment required within a year.

Japanization

Once order was established, Japanese authorities set about imprinting Japanese culture on Singapore, a process known as *Japanization*, to erase Britain's colonial legacy. The name was immediately changed from Singapore to Syonan-to, meaning *Light of the South*, reflecting Singapore's status as the capital of the southern region of Japan's possessions. The Georgian calendar used by the Europeans was changed to the Imperial Calendar of Japan, which counts years from the traditional date of Japan's founding in 660 B.C.E., so 1942 became 2602. The time zone was also altered so Singapore would be on the same time as Tokyo. A new currency was introduced; the names of public offices, such as the courts, and newspapers were given Japanese names.

Language was a main focus of the program's efforts; because officials hoped Japanese would replace English as the language of common use, although they realized this would take some time. There was a public campaign to teach people *katakana*, a simplified, phonetic Japanese writing system; and there were incentives for people to learn Japanese, including preferences for job hiring. Schools were gradually reopened after a few months of occupation, and a Japanese-oriented curriculum was introduced with hours of language instruction each day.

Authorities also sought to instill in people the "Japanese spirit" that reflected the greatness of the nation. Each day there were flag and anthem ceremonies and compulsory fitness drills set to music from Japanese radio. The Emperor's birthday became a holiday. School children began each day by facing toward Japan and singing patriotic songs. People were also required to bow to officials from the Imperial administration. To underscore their elite status, there were certain elevators in some office buildings that only Japanese could use and two of Singapore's main department stores were closed to non-Japanese customers. As a further effort to remove the European stamp from Singapore, western music, film, and theater were prohibited with few exceptions.

Difficulties of Daily Life under Occupation

As is common during wartime, especially in an import-based economy, shortages soon became a reality for most Singaporeans. Families in good standing with the administration received Peace Living Certificates that entitled them to ration cards for items such as rice, meat, sugar, salt, and other essentials. The situation worsened as the tide of war turned against Japan and resources, including food, became scarce. A thriving black market developed, so people were able to supplement their rations in that manner, but that depended on wealth, especially as prices and shortages increased. Creative substitutions were found, for example, tapioca was used to make bread once wheat flour became unavailable. However, not all of these were adequate dietary substitutions; and incidents of malnutrition and related illnesses, such as beriberi caused by B-vitamin deficiency, became more prevalent.

To help overcome shortages, increase Singapore's self-sufficiency, and reduce the need for imports, the Japanese administration initiated a program in which available green spaces were converted to gardens, which residents were expected to work. The program was promoted through the schools and government-controlled media. However, Singapore's soil had never been very good for cultivation and little came of the efforts.

The Japanese also took other measures to try to deal with the commodity shortages. Since refugees from the Malay Peninsula had increased the population, the Japanese initially encouraged, and then later ordered, people to return home. They also set up a couple of commune-type villages, one in Johor and one farther north, to which they encouraged people to move and become self-sufficient through farming. There was some incentive to go, because people gained distance from the watchful eye of the Japanese administration and military police; plus the administration promised to provide most of the resources to get started. The settlement in Johor that was populated mostly by ethnic Chinese and received support from the Oversea Chinese Association did well and was able to grow a lot of food. The other, comprised mainly of Christian professionals who did not have good farming skills and had worse land and fewer resources than the Johor settlement, failed to prosper, and a number of the participants died. None of the efforts to reduce Singapore's population were very successful, and there remained too many mouths to feed from the available food. Food scarcity grew severe toward the end of the war, and people had to stand in long lines to get basic items such as rice.

The food shortages were exacerbated by rampant inflation that resulted from the disorganized approach the Japanese took to introduce the new currency. Its value was not properly supported, and, while the first bills issued had serial numbers, successive printings did not, making them easy to counterfeit. Inflation was a problem from the beginning. The mandated Chinese gift helped take currency out of circulation and helped steady the value for a time, but that was short-lived. The Japanese then introduced a lottery that appealed to many people, helped take still more currency out of circulation, and also helped finance the Japanese war effort. A further attempt was a succession of savings campaigns in which officials encouraged people to save their money. Ultimately, however, the inflation continued to rise. The situation was worse in Singapore than on the Malay Peninsula, where food was one-half to one-third less expensive. Real estate was likewise extremely inflated and a property that cost $5,000 to $6,000 before the war increased to prices ranging from $160,000 to $250,000 by March 1945.[18]

An additional problem was widespread corruption. The low value of money due to inflation led to a cavalier attitude, in which money was easily made and spent. Bribes, extortion, and protection money schemes were commonplace and considered a cost of doing business. It was in the corrupt business of the black market in which much of the economic activity took place. The formal economy was Japanese dominated, with Japanese corporations such as Mitsubishi having taken over the major industries of shipping, rubber, tin, and others. Non-Japanese people needed a special permit to conduct such trade. Some enterprising Singaporeans, in particular some members of the Chinese community who were well-connected from their past roles as intermediate brokers, were able to find new wealth despite this, typically through the black market. For political reasons, there was often a Japanese person as the face of the operation, but that was usually just a front in the survival economy. Black market goods met so many needs that dealing on the black market became a necessity, and the scale of business was large.

Daily life became harder in all aspects as the war drew to its end. Food and other commodities became ever scarcer; Japanese authorities became less predictable and increasingly harsh; the money became ever lower in value. At the same time, the censorship of the press prevented people from receiving accurate news reports about the progress of the war. Short-wave radios that could pick up the British

Broadcasting Corporation (BBC) transmissions had been banned, so very few people had them. However, by July 1945, Allied aircraft were overflying Singapore daily and people realized the end was near. There was also considerable bombing of the port. Civilians and Japanese authorities assumed that there could be a second Battle of Singapore, which led to hoarding of commodities by authorities, aggravating the shortages, and increasing anxiety among civilians. Lacking replacement parts, important aspects of the infrastructure like electricity production also started to fail. The situation had become miserable for most of the population.

The United States dropped atomic bombs on Japan on August 6 and 9, 1945. On August 15, Emperor Hirohito officially announced Japan's surrender, which was broadcast over radio around Japan. It was finally announced in Singapore's media on August 21. The Japanese began preparing their own internment camp at Jurong as they waited for Allied forces to land. On September 2, British and Commonwealth troops arrived and received a warm welcome from the population. The Singaporeans had a new, humbler view of the British, but British rule had been less brutal than that of the Japanese occupiers, so the British were welcomed. On September 12, Japanese army and navy officials in Singapore officially and publicly surrendered to Lord Louis Mountbattan, the Supreme Allied Commander of Southeast Asia. The Japanese military leaders who controlled Singapore's fate during the war met different ends. Tsuji, the planner of the invasion, slipped away to China and hid out until the British ended attempts to put him on trial. He made his way back to Japan and was eventually elected to the Japanese parliament. Yamashita, the general who became known as the Tiger of Malaya for his successful sweep down the Peninsula, was stationed in the Philippines at the end of the war and was captured by the Americans. He was the first of the Japanese generals to be tried for war crimes and was executed in February 1946.

The experience of shocking defeat and painful occupation left a lasting mark on Singapore. To the local population, British control was supposed to mean protection, but the British had failed profoundly. The Singapore to which the British returned was not the same Singapore they had left. The people's trust had been compromised and they were prepared to consider a different future.

NOTES

1. Karl Hack and Kevin Blackburn, *Did Singapore Have to Fall?* (New York, NY: Routledge Curzon, 2004), 40.

2. C. M. Turnbull, *A History of Singapore, 1819–1988*, 2nd ed. (New York, NY: Oxford University Press, 1989), 159–160.

3. Malcolm Murfett et al., *Between Two Oceans* (New York, NY: Marshall Cavendish International, 2004), 190.

4. A. W. King, "Plantation and Agriculture in Malaya, with Notes on the Trade of Singapore," *The Geographical Journal*, 39 (1939), 136–148.

5. Hack and Blackburn, *Did Singapore Have to Fall?* 148.

6. Murfett et al., *Between Two Oceans*, 220–221.

7. Ibid., 264.

8. Ibid., 269.

9. C. M. Turnbull, *A History of Singapore*, 181.

10. Hack and Blackburn, *Did Singapore Have to Fall?* 5.

11. Murfett et al., *Between Two Oceans*, 321.

12. Ibid., 328.

13. C. M. Turnbull, *A History of Singapore*, 188.

14. D. O. W. Hall. "Prisoners of Japan: The Burma-Thailand Railway," New Zealand Electronic Text Centre, http://www.nzetc.org/tm/scholarly/tei-WH2-1Epi-c6-WH2-1Epi-f.html.

15. Murfett et al., *Between Two Oceans*, 308.

16. Ibid., 306 and National Heritage Board. "Sook Ching Centre," Heritage Trails, http://heritagetrails.sg/content/586/Sook_Ching_Centre.html.

17. C. M. Turnbull, *A History of Singapore*, 195.

18. Ibid., 199–200.

6

The Rough Road to Independence: 1945–1963

When World War II abruptly ended with the U.S. atomic bombing of Japan, Britain returned to administer its restored colony. However, there was understanding on both Singaporean and British sides that they could not return to the pre-war situation. Already in 1943, the British Colonial Office began planning for the gradual shift from British control to self-governance for the Straits Settlements, although the sudden end of the war left the British without a finalized plan and the primary focus for self-government was on the Malay states; Singapore could continue as a crown colony indefinitely. The following years proved tumultuous, and the future that many in Singapore envisioned was one where Singapore was a part of Malaysia. Once the initial years of post-war recovery passed, a communist insurgency on the Malay Peninsula resulted in a state of emergency; and there was a separate, but likewise problematic, attempt by communists in Singapore to gain control of the country. New political forces eventually put down the communist threat and the dream of merging with Malaysia was briefly realized but failed in the face of incompatibility.

The independent country of Singapore was born. While much of what transpired related to group dynamics in Singapore and even in Malaysia, the events took place within the larger context of the global Cold War struggle between communism and capitalism.

THE POST-WAR RECOVERY

Control of Singapore, both military and civilian aspects, was in the hands of the British Military Administration (BMA), which was under the direction of Supreme Allied Commander of Southeast Asia Lord Louis Mountbattan. While Singaporeans initially welcomed the British, who were certain to be less abusive than the Japanese occupiers, the situation after the war was direr than people had hoped. Some of the problems were due to ongoing shortages of food and other necessities. Shipping was difficult; the port had been badly damaged in Allied bombings and needed to be rebuilt and re-equipped, because cranes, dredgers, and other essential machinery had been destroyed or were missing. In addition, the harbor was partially blocked by sunken ships, and most warehouses had been ruined. Even the railroad coming from the Malay Peninsula was damaged, making the import of goods into Singapore very difficult. Worse still, rice-producing countries faced shortages themselves and were not exporting. The prices of available goods were inflated, contributing further to supply shortages. Beyond transportation and food scarcity, further suffering was related to the dilapidated infrastructure in areas of water, electricity, etc. Housing was also a grave problem. There was overcrowding in the urban center before the war, but with the destruction from bombing and the inflation in real estate prices that happened during the Japanese occupation, many people resorted to living in casually erected slums that lacked sanitation. Between the unclean living conditions and malnutrition from the food shortages, the mortality rate in 1945 doubled from its pre-war level.[1]

Further problems were credited to mismanagement and corruption in the lower ranks of the BMA. The climate of the occupation, where rules were ignored in the name of survival, spilled over into the reconstruction era. The black market continued to thrive, as did bribery and other forms of corruption. It continued in the police, who had lost all legitimate authority during the occupation, and in the government with a new cast of players in the BMA. There were few British administrators who were not new to Singapore. The earlier staffers were recovering from their time as internees or prisoners of war, leaving the government primarily staffed with new people, many of whom capitalized on Singapore's thriving black market and on other opportunities such as bribes for travel permits, trade licenses, etc. While the upper echelons of the BMA were generally honest, the lower levels were so corrupt that the local population called the BMA the Black Market Administration. The BMA also implemented a number of policies, including rationing and price setting to help mitigate food scarcity and inflation. While these policies were not corrupt, they were not effective immediately, and the shortages and high prices continued unabated. Between corruption and inefficiency, the British administration lost all respect in the eyes of the people. The BMA's efforts to prosecute the Japanese for war crimes further exacerbated the people's disappointment. Trials relating to crimes against civilian internees and military prisoners of war resulted in some convictions. However, the effort to try the perpetrators of the *sook ching*, which cost many thousands of Chinese lives, proved more problematic. A series of trials did result in a couple of executions and some life sentences, but the Chinese community felt the administration had put more effort into the trials involving crimes against British or Commonwealth citizens than those involving Chinese victims.

Other social problems, including gambling, prostitution, and opium use, continued from the occupation era. The black market, bribery, and profiteering flourished in the private sector as much as it did in the public sector. In addition, the secret societies began to thrive again.

On a more positive note, the BMA reopened schools in a timely manner. It moved quickly to restore the port and infrastructure; and by April 1946, the port was almost back to normal, and more people had access to water and electricity than before the war. It also did a good job of removing corrupt and tainted police officials and launching a new police recruiting effort. Moreover, within six months or so, the rationing policies began to work, and food shortages became less severe. While the slow progress disappointed the population, the BMA made important improvements in a relatively short time before being replaced by Colonial Office governance in April 1946.

One major legacy of the BMA was a policy related to communist activity. The pre-war colonial administration, seeing communist influences from China as a threat, had taken actions such as banning local Chinese Communist Party branches in Singapore. In response, the Malay Communist Party (MCP) was born in 1930, which the British also attempted to suppress. However, the group that emerged from the war with the greatest respect was, in fact, the MCP. While there was virtually no active resistance in Singapore during occupation, on the Malay Peninsula, the MCP created the Malayan People's Anti-Japanese Army (MPAJA). The MPAJA was comprised mostly of ethnic Chinese people from both Singapore and cities in the Malay Peninsula who fled to the jungles and fought with guerilla tactics against the occupying Japanese. People of varying ideologies participated; but by the end of the war, the MPAJA was closely linked to and heavily populated by communists. The Chinese community felt the British did not afford adequate respect to the fighters as the sole resistance to the abusive Japanese, which caused more resentment. The MCP decommissioned the MPAJA a few months after the occupation ended and decided to use political tactics to promote its agenda of independence from British colonial rule.

In order to recruit for their cause, the MCP opted to organize through labor unions and in opposition to the BMA. The BMA initially recognized the status of the MCP, but when the MCP (and the affiliated unions it quickly and easily organized) began planning strikes and rallies, the organization attracted negative attention from authorities. There was considerable disagreement within the BMA about how to react. Mountbattan preferred a more lenient approach, permitting greater freedom of speech and assembly, but other top officials strongly disagreed and wanted a harsher response. Some restrictions were in place, but several major actions were allowed to take place, including a general strike opposing the unfair detention of a guerilla fighter in January 1946 that involved almost 173,000 people.[2] However, when it was announced that the unions wanted to have another major action a few weeks later on February 15 to commemorate the start of occupation (or "the day the white men ran," as the Malays called it[3]), the British reacted with less tolerance, suggesting that observing the end of occupation would be more appropriate and issuing a warning of detention and, for noncitizens (the majority of the Chinese community), possible deportation. The MCP went ahead with their planning. Mountbattan worried about making martyrs out of activists but relented, and ten labor organizers were detained and later deported to a *Guomindang* stronghold in southern China, where they would have met with great difficulties because of their communist affiliations. This set the stage for more than a decade of focused and sometimes harsh anticommunist activity carried out first by the Colonial Office and then by local authorities in Malaysia and Singapore.

STATE OF EMERGENCY AND STEPS TOWARD SELF-GOVERNANCE

The economic situation slowly improved with trade reaching prewar levels in 1947, and rubber production surpassing the war-time high in 1948.[4] However, in the sultanates of the Malay Peninsula, the political situation took a problematic turn. The Colonial Office was interested in a close union of the different states/sultanates on the Peninsula, but Singapore was excluded. The two, in the mind of the Colonial Office, were not compatible, despite being connected geographically, economically, and historically. The deal-breaking factor was ethnicity, with Singapore having a large majority of ethnic Chinese while the Malay sultanates had a slight Malay majority. The Colonial Office feared the two would not mix well; if citizens wanted union in the future, it could happen, but not for the time being. A political alliance of Malay traditional elites, known as the United Malays National Organization (UMNO), came to an agreement with wealthy Malay Chinese elites (the Malay Chinese Association) to oppose the Colonial Office plans. The Malay sultans wanted more power for themselves in a federation and the Chinese elite did not like Singapore's exclusion. The Malay Federation would form, but Singapore's steps toward self-governance would proceed more gradually.

The MCP was impatient with the slow pace toward self-governance set by the British and, unhappy with the plan of separation, began an anticolonial insurgency on the Peninsula in June 1948. The organization had a vision of an urban communist revolution in Singapore, but that became secondary to the armed struggle in the Malay states. The British responded by declaring a state of emergency in both the Malay states and in Singapore, which lasted for 12 years. The fighting on the Malay Peninsula against the "communist terrorists," as they were known, never touched Singapore directly, but there were profound political implications in the restrictions associated with the state of emergency.

The British goal was to withdraw from Southeast Asia, leaving in place friendly, malleable governments, which would want to be members of the Commonwealth, and would, thus, still help serve and promote the substantial British interests in the region. Among these ongoing interests were banks, insurance companies, and trading companies, in addition to the rubber, tin, and shipping industries. Military installations, the Sembawang Naval Base, plus airfields and an army base, were also major interests that would help maintain Britain's prominence on the world stage. All of this played out against the backdrop of the Cold War. The United States was involved more directly in Vietnam and the Philippines, but its Containment Policy, one of the most significant U.S. foreign policies of the Cold War era, focused on limiting the spread of communism; and the United States was reluctant to see any colonies come under the rule of communist, or even neutral, governments. As such, the United States promoted entities in

Singapore (certain schools, unions, newspapers, and people within the Singapore Chinese Chamber of Commerce) with connections to the *Guomindang* government that took refuge in Taiwan after the Chinese Communist Party took over China in 1949. The United States also planted anticommunist propaganda pieces in the Singaporean media and pressed Britain to take action against communist activities. Of primary concern in all of this was the Chinese community.

Singapore served as a base for Britain's fight against the communist insurgency on the Peninsula, with Sembawang Naval Base supporting Royal Navy patrols of the Malay coasts and the airbases facilitating bombing sorties. The British brought the population in the Malay states into the struggle by moving the schedule for independence ahead to 1957, thus giving the people a vested interest in the fight for the future of their country. The British fight against the communists was successful. While the state of emergency lasted until 1960, the insurgency was put down earlier, giving birth to the Malay Federation as an independent state on August 31, 1957. The dominant political force in the federation was the conservative, anticommunist UMNO, which promoted nationalist policies favoring the Malay ethnic group and focused on ethnic differentiation rather than solidarity.

In Singapore, most of the effects of the state of emergency were political. The declaration of emergency permitted considerable restrictions on political freedoms, including detention without charges or trial, deportation of noncitizens, and restrictions on meetings, rallies, strikes, organizations, etc. The anticommunist focus stifled all left-leaning politics and left space only for conservative political organizations. This happened at a time when local political organizations were beginning to flourish in Singapore. A new array of organizations representing a wide range of the political spectrum, from the left-oriented MCP and Malay Democratic Union to the moderately conservative Singapore Progressive Party (SPP), a group associated with the colonial administration that did not promote any progressive social, economic or political changes. The British administration was slowly opening the door to popular representation on the Legislative Council, heightening the importance of local political parties.

Believing the institutional reforms leading to elected seats on the council did not go far, or fast, enough to move Singapore toward independence, many leftward political actors opposed the reforms. As such, the Malay Democratic Union boycotted the 1948 election for the new Legislative Council seats. Formal political participation (e.g., voting) was restricted to people born in the Straits, British subjects, and those literate in English, which excluded more than half of the adult population of immigrant Chinese, numbering into the hundreds of thousands. The Asians with access to political participation were the English-educated elite, who tended to be more conservative and accepting of the slow pace toward self-government (of a still undetermined form) for Singapore. As space in the Legislative Council opened, the only political organization contesting the election was the SPP. Much to the delight of the British administration, the SPP proved a cooperative partner in the council. However, the British were naively unaware of how unrepresentative the views of the SPP were and how disconnected the SPP was from the Asian masses in Singapore, which tended to see the SPP as the lapdog of the colonial master. The emergency provisions and targeting of left-leaning political groups deprived the community of a potential safety valve for venting frustration with the status quo. The Malay Democratic Union disbanded in the face of anticommunist pressure from the government and the frustrations of the voiceless masses grew.

There were a number of political issues of importance to the majority of people living in Singapore, and these issues were neither addressed by the colonial administration nor advocated on the Legislative Council by the SPP. One of the top political issues was citizenship reform aimed at giving the majority of the Chinese population a political voice. The Singapore Chinese Chamber of Commerce launched a campaign for this goal in 1951, but the British administration, supported by the SPP, refused to enact reform.

Another contentious issue was the education system. The British had increased financial support for schools in order to develop the citizenship skills necessary for successful self-governance. However, the administration allowed the funding to follow demand, which tended heavily toward English-medium education. In fact, four times the number of students now enrolled in English-medium schools than before the war.[5] The pay for teachers in Chinese-medium schools was far less than those in English-medium schools and the educational options were limited with only a few secondary and no post-secondary Chinese-medium schools. This left Chinese-medium students with few options to continue their schooling, so many chose to go to the People's Republic of China to further their education. This was problematic due to the anticommunist immigration policy in place in the colony, which banned any immigrants with communist connections. Thus, Chinese-educated young people, most of whom were residents (rather than citizens) and had limited political rights, could go to China, but they could not come home to Singapore and their families. The supporters of the Chinese-medium schools saw the funding disparities, the underdeveloped Chinese education system, and the anti-immigrant policies as signs that the British wanted to destroy the Chinese school system, thereby undermining Chinese language and culture, which provoked ire. This came at a time when the Chinese community was especially attuned to the political developments in China, which sparked a heightened sense of patriotism even among noncommunists; and they were, thus, angered by what they perceived as British hostility toward Chinese patriotism. It was also at a time when the Chinese community was feeling renewed strength from the increased wealth flowing in from the trade that expanded greatly with the start of the Korean War in 1950. A strong resentment developed toward paying taxes to support programs and schools that undermined the Chinese community, language, culture, and even families.

A third major issue was the question of language and, specifically, multilingualism. The British authorities, with ongoing support from the mostly-English-educated SPP, promoted English as the language of the colony. The Chinese community advocated for the Chinese language to be elevated in status and for all four of the major languages—Chinese, English, Malay, and Tamil—to be used in proceedings of the Legislative Council as well as municipal organizations.

Finally, the fourth problematic issue was the racial composition of the civil service and other important employment venues, which were still overtly racist in their hiring and promotion practices. In a community that was supposed to be advancing toward self-governance but where the local population still suffered gross discrimination in job opportunities, it was unacceptable that the civil service be staffed heavily by Europeans. Thus, quickly staffing the ranks of the civil service and other organizations with Asians was a top priority for the Asian communities. Historian Carl Trocki noted that, "... as late as 1954, ... the British governor of Singapore, Sir John Nicoll, would not hire an equally qualified Asian over a European."[6]

Relatively unaware of these simmering tensions, the British administration continued to take slow steps toward self-governance, without addressing critical issues. The year 1953 was important in several respects. First, the Rendel Commission was appointed to evaluate the political and constitutional structures of Singapore that would help Singapore move toward self-governance in a still-to-be-determined context. Second, the struggle against the insurgency on the Malay Peninsula was going well, and the government relaxed of some of the harsh restrictions on political activities in Singapore. While the Rendel Commission worked, the Malay Communist Party was busy redirecting its efforts toward Singapore and infiltrated Chinese schools and unions. The frustrations of the disenfranchised Chinese, both with the poor school system and poor working conditions, proved a fertile environment for communist recruitment and, beginning in 1954, Singapore was struck with recurrent waves of political violence. Especially problematic for the British was that the student protesters and labor activists joined forces, broadening the focus of the protests from better educational opportunities and improved workers rights to a radicalized anti-British and anticolonial movement. They viewed the incremental steps toward an unclear political future offered by the British, and controlled by pro-British, English-educated elites, as intolerable. The British offered education reform and improved funding for Chinese-medium schools but with conditions attached relating to oversight of school management on issues such as curriculum. The conditions were met with anger in the Chinese community. The British also tried to promote noncommunist union organizations, which likewise came to naught. Instead, student and labor protests grew; and it was rumored that two of the leading organizers connected to both groups, Lim Chin Siong and Fong Swee Suan, could bring Singapore to a halt through protest action on any day of their choosing.

In this increasingly hostile climate, the Rendel Commission issued its recommendations. It called for a Legislative Assembly based on geographical constituencies rather than ethnic lines (ethnic-based representation had been advocated by the British earlier but found little favor with the Asian representatives who wanted cross-communal politics) with 25 of the 32 seats being elected and the others appointed. A Council of Ministers would replace the old colonial Executive Committee of advisors to the governor. Two-thirds of the council's members would be selected by the leader of the strongest party in the Legislative Assembly and the other third would be appointed by the governor. This new government would have authority over all areas except foreign, internal security, and defense policies. The British government accepted the commission's recommendations, and arrangements were made for an election for the Legislative Assembly to be held in 1955.

THE 1955 ELECTION AND ITS AFTERMATH

Although many in the Chinese community lacked voting rights, the remainder, when mobilized, was enough to sway an election. The political parties that emerged in the new electoral environment were varied. On the conservative side, the SPP remained to contest the election and was joined by the Democratic Party, formed by some members of the Singapore Chinese Chamber of Commerce and representing narrow Chinese business interests.

Two major political forces emerged on the left: the socialist Labour Front (LF) led by lawyer David Marshall, and the People's Action Party (PAP), a group of English-educated, middle-class professionals, led by lawyer Lee Kwan Yew. The PAP would ultimately become the dominant force in Singaporean political life. Lee's background was not radical; he had been involved with the SPP before leaving the party because he found its vision too narrow. He had done legal work for unions, bringing him into contact with union organizers and people with grievances against the racist hiring and promotion practices of the British. He considered the best path to political power was to tap into the masses of left-leaning workers, especially, but not exclusively, in the Chinese community. The PAP called for an immediate merger of Singapore with the Malay Federation, citizenship reform to permit the naturalization of hundreds of thousands of disenfranchised Chinese, civil service reform to staff it fully with Asians, the repeal of the emergency restrictions, free and compulsory education, a focus on the development of local industry, and legislative reform relating to unions.

The election took place, with the automatic registration of voters increasing the voting rosters from 76,000 to 300,000, most of whom were Chinese blue-collar workers.[7] The Labour Front won the largest number of seats, but not a majority, leaving Marshall in a difficult position in two respects. First, as leader of the strongest party in the Legislative Assembly, he assumed the brand new role of Chief Minister (similar to a prime minister); but the role and its powers were not clearly defined relative to those of the colonial governor, who was supposed to receive the chief minister's advice but was not bound to act on it. That Governor Nicoll intended to marginalize Marshall was clear from the fact that Marshall was not given office space until he threatened to set up a desk outside in front of the building. Even afterward, his was just a small office underneath the stairs. The second problem was the lack of a legislative majority, creating a reliance on opposition party support to pass legislation and carry out the LF agenda. This agenda was remarkably similar to that of the PAP, calling for the immediate independence of Singapore and merger with the Malay Federation, citizenship reform, Asian staffing of the civil service within four years, abolition of the emergency regulations, and the introduction of all four languages for use in the Legislative Assembly.

Marshall quickly ran into difficulties, much of them dealing with increasing communist activism, some of it violent. One of the most notorious incidents of this tumultuous period came just a few weeks after the election with the Hock Lee Bus Strike, which lasted for almost three weeks before escalating into rioting in which a handful of people were killed and dozens injured. Bus company workers started the protest, but were soon joined by students from Chinese schools. Initially, Marshall responded somewhat moderately, as he had sympathies for the causes of the student and labor protesters. This restraint alienated the British, who wanted a stronger response, and empowered the protesters for further action. At one point, thousands of Chinese secondary school students protested to gain recognition of their student union. Marshall agreed, although with the stipulation that they not engage in political activities. They agreed but broke the promise. While the unrest touched all of society, it profoundly affected the PAP, which was deeply divided between its moderate branch led by Lee Kwan Yew and the militant, communist branch led by Lim Chin Siong, who was a leader in organizing protest activities. Marshall accused the PAP of trying to undermine rule by representative government in favor of mob rule. Indeed, many of the strikes had more to do with political than labor issues. In 1955, of the approximately 300 strikes, it is estimated that only one-third related to labor issues like wages or working conditions.[8]

Marshall used the unrest to push the British government for more power for the chief minister. Initially reluctant, once Marshall threatened to resign, the British conceded for fear that someone more militant would gain the position. This highlights some of Marshall's most significant accomplishments as chief minister: despite the British intent to treat him like a figurehead, he forced the British to take him and the local politicians seriously. He also launched the LF's legislative agenda on civil service and citizenship reform.

However, it was in the climate of communist-led turmoil that a meeting took place in April 1956 in London about making additional changes to Singapore's constitutional status and moving it further toward self-governance. Marshall had a list of demands, and the British were amenable to many of them. However, they held firm on maintaining a strong hand in internal security matters; and Marshall was not willing to compromise his goal of achieving complete internal governance by 1957, the time of projected Malay independence. He returned to Singapore empty-handed and resigned as head of the LF a short time later. He was replaced by the deputy chief minister, Lim

Yew Hock, who created a high degree of governmental continuity by retaining Marshall's cabinet and maintaining the LF's alliances.

Lim Yew Hock was less tolerant of the communist protests and soon cracked down on activists in the schools. In September 1956, he ordered the disbanding of a number of communist school organizations, closed several schools, and had some students expelled. The PAP's Lim Chin Siong helped organize a 5,000-student sit-in at six different Chinese schools. When no one could get students to leave, the police used tear gas. Rioting broke out around the city; and in the end, 15 people were dead, 100 injured, and Singapore was placed under curfew for two days.[9] Documents found in a related raid on a union headquarters confirmed the connections between the student and labor agitation, resulting in the arrest of several leaders, including Lim Chin Siong.

This challenge to the communists helped undermine the movement and put Lim Yew Hock in favor with the British, who found evidence in the rioting that the communist threat was real and that the PAP was involved. This left Lim Yew Hock in a better position for the next round of meetings on Singapore's constitutional status in London in March 1957. Lim Yew Hock was more willing to compromise than Marshall, and they came to an agreement on the internal security arrangements that had been a stumbling block previously. The outcome was an Internal Security Council composed of three British members, three Singaporean members and one member from the Malay Federation. The other provisions the British had offered the previous year were accepted and Singapore was one step closer to self-government, although the question of its relationship to the Malay Federation remained. Other crucial provisions included a fully elected assembly (no appointed members), a special provision for citizenship for long-term resident Chinese, and control of trade and commerce.

The communists were unhappy when news of the Internal Security Council reached Singapore. With three British members and one Malay member, the Council was dominated by anticommunists. Seeking more radical action, communists tried to mobilize via the MCP and radicals at Nanyang University, a new Chinese-language university that had been funded with private contributions from all echelons of the Chinese community in effort to improve education opportunities for students in the Chinese-medium schools as an alternative to studying in China. The MCP and Nanyang mobilization targeted the unions and the moderates in the PAP.

Lim Yew Hock, concerned about the new wave of militant behavior, started another campaign against communist radicalism, especially in the unions, even though some of them supported his own Labour Front. Inadvertently, he did a favor to the moderate wing of the PAP that was battling for survival within the party. When the PAP communists were jailed, the moderates received a life-sustaining boost and promptly re-wrote party policies to make it harder for extremists to influence the top levels of the party, marginalizing them at the lower levels.

Progress was made on a number of the political agenda items important to the Chinese community. Staffing the civil service with members of the three Asian communities was proceeding apace. Citizenship was granted to anyone who had been born in Singapore or the Malay Federation, or British citizens who had been in Singapore for two years, or those who had been there for at least ten years and would swear loyalty to Singapore. This gave voting rights to most of the previously excluded 220,000 immigrant Chinese. Finally, education reform gave equal status to the school systems in each of the four languages.

In this environment of greater stability and political progress, the third London meeting about Singapore's constitutional status took place in April 1958, which largely confirmed and formalized the arrangements of the prior year. In August the British Parliament passed the State of Singapore Act, which converted its status from colony to state, albeit a semi-sovereign state lacking control over all of its affairs, with Britain retaining control over foreign relations, external defense, and, in an emergency, the right to suspend the constitution. However, all other decisions would be in the hands of the local government, an enormous step toward self-governance. This act of parliament set the stage for the implementation of the new arrangements, necessitating the selection of a new, fully-elected Legislative Assembly so an election was planned for 1959.

THE 1959 ELECTION AND THE ROAD TO MERGER

While the PAP only made a mediocre showing in the 1955 election, it vowed to do better in 1959. Seeing its voting base in the masses of working-class Chinese, the PAP had weekly rallies. After the Labour Front collapsed in the face of a scandal, the PAP candidates wore white clothing to symbolize their political purity. The party promised clean, efficient politics and pledged to address issues in education, labor, housing, health, social security, economic growth through industrialization, and merger with the Malay Federation as a pathway to full independence from Britain. The PAP swept the election, winning 43 of 51 seats in the Legislative Assembly.

The PAP victory terrified many conservatives since the party had been associated closely with militant communist action through party leaders like Lim Chin Siong. In many people's minds, the PAP was still linked with that radicalism, despite the extremists being in jail. Although having moderate roots and having established cordial relations with the British authorities, Lee Kwan Yew also had a record of inflammatory rhetoric and thus was little differentiated from the more extreme Lim Chin Siong and other party leaders known for their anti-capitalist speech and behavior. Anxiety in the business community led companies to move their headquarters from Singapore to Kuala Lumpur, the capital of the Malay Federation, which caused capital flight and falling property prices. Given Singapore's ongoing reliance on international capital, this was a problem. Lee Kwan Yew did not help the situation when he insisted on the release of some of the jailed PAP leaders and then gave them positions in the government, albeit minor ones well away from the center of power.

The PAP's answer to the capital flight problem was twofold. First, leaders envisioned a new economic plan that focused on industrializing Singapore. This was appealing for a number of reasons. The economy had flourished with the onset of the Korean War in 1950, but when the fighting stopped in 1953, so did the revenue from war-related demand. Unemployment levels were extremely high, feeding support for communism. Singapore's economy was still heavily based on entrepôt trade, especially rubber, which comprised two-thirds of Singapore's exports during the 1950s, half supplied from the Malay Peninsula and half from Indonesia. In 1960, Singapore was the world's largest exporter of rubber.[10] However, the 1950s had been a difficult time for the rubber trade with unsteady supplies and prices. Worse, the future of the rubber trade looked more uncertain as the newly independent Malay Federation was likely to develop its own ports and trade. Further, President Sukarno of Indonesia was promoting economic nationalism by insisting that Indonesian goods be traded only through Indonesian ports. The uneven levels of trade in the 1950s exacerbated the economic difficulties of high unemployment, which was also fed in part by Singapore's birth rate, one of the world's highest. The lesson Singapore's leaders took from this was that entrepôt trade was unreliable and could not provide security and improved quality of life for the people. Singapore needed new economic opportunities, and industrialization was the government's choice.

The second approach to addressing the capital flight after the PAP election was to push for a rapid merger with the Malay Federation. This would help the Singaporean economy in several ways. First, if

Singapore were part of the federation, the rubber supply would likely be more reliable. Second, until Singapore was within a common market with the federation, something Singaporeans expected to come with merger, Singapore would be on the wrong side of Malay trade barriers. Finally, with the hope of new industrialization being the path to stability, full employment, and release from poverty, Singapore needed a larger domestic market for its goods.

Lee Kwon Yew also made it clear that he saw merger as a key to controlling the communists. A Chinese proverb says when you ride the tiger, it is hard to get off, lest you get eaten. When he affiliated himself with the likes of Lim Chin Siong and his followers to gain political support from the Chinese masses, Lee Kwan Yew climbed on the tiger. Now he had to control it. He said that he could not challenge the communists as long as the British still had some control over Singapore; if he did, he would look like a puppet of the British and the communists would appear as "anti-colonial martyrs,"[11] but with merger, the conservative, anticommunist Malay government could help address the communist threat. He also expressed his concern that without merger, Singapore could become an organizational base for communist forces working in opposition to the ideologically nationalist Malay government.

Singapore's difficult relationship with the Malay Federation was at the center of the merger agenda. Despite Lee Kwan Yew's warning to Malay leaders that Singapore may be a threat outside the federation, they were alarmed by the level of communist activism in Singapore since 1953, especially since they had just gotten the upper hand on the communist guerilla insurgency on the Peninsula. Moreover, while Singapore and the federation were united by geography, history, and economics, they were divided in other meaningful ways. They had been evolving along different trajectories since the end of World War II, and very different political and social philosophies had developed. In the Malay Federation, the strong political force of Malay nationalism had manifested itself in a preference system that advantaged Malays over members of other ethnic groups. For example, a civil service quota required four Malays for each non-Malay employee. Malays were disadvantaged in economic power (held mostly by ethnic Chinese in the federation), so they were deliberate about protecting political power for ethnic Malays. Malay was the official language, and other Asian languages had no legal status. In contrast, in Singapore, there was less focus on ethnicity in politics. While there had been conflict over English-medium versus Chinese-medium schools, no political party advocated benefits for one ethnic group over another; in fact, with the official multilingualism in the Legislative Assembly and the official equality of each of the four language streams in education, Singapore had moved in the opposite direction of the Malay leaders on a fundamental issue for ethnically diverse societies. Moreover, the nature of Malay nationalism had an anti-Chinese element to it, which was problematic when the population of Singapore had a strong Chinese majority. The ethnic composition of the two states was at the crux of the concerns of the Malay leaders. The 1957 census revealed that of the Malay Federation's population of 6,279,000, 50 percent was Malay and 37 percent Chinese, while Singapore's 1,446,000 people were 75 percent Chinese and 13 percent Malay.[12] Moreover, Singapore's citizenship laws were more liberal than the federation's, making it far easier for ethnic Chinese to gain citizenship. The Malay leaders feared the dilution of Malay political power in the case of a merger. Between the communist activities and the threat to Malay nationalism, the Malay Federation opposed merger in 1959 and the years prior. With a seat on the Internal Security Council, the Malay Federation already had a voice in protecting itself from security problems that might arise from Singapore and this voice, combined with the unwavering anticommunism of the British, would suffice.

The state of emergency was officially rescinded in 1960, suggesting a lesser communist threat, and the PAP made efforts to reach out to and reassure Malay leaders. The PAP leadership made it clear that it was unimaginable to have a separate future from the Malay Federation, and even before taking power in 1959, had tried to demonstrate their cooperativeness. In 1954 the PAP created a party Bureau for Malay Affairs; in 1956 it advocated for a common school system to build ties between the two populations. In 1959, when Singapore was able to have its first non-British head of state (a largely ceremonial position), the person picked was a Malay. The PAP leaders recognized Malay as the national language. They especially targeted the Singaporean Malay community for social development programs, including more schools and community centers. The PAP's main focus, though, was to advance society and bridge differences between groups through social and economic development; it was not a differentiating communal approach like that found in the federation.

On the economic front, the PAP attempted to make advances. For example, in 1961, the government established an Economic Development Program focused on import-substitution industrialization, a development approach that calls for the creation and then protection of domestic industries that will produce goods for the home market that would otherwise be imported. One initiative was the development of an industrial park in Jurong on what had been 4,000 acres of swampland. Based on advice from the World Bank, the plan for the park offered a range of tax incentives and tax breaks for both local and foreign investors as well as tariffs to protect the goods produced there. The hope was that labor-intensive industry, such as textiles, would decrease the high level of unemployment. Lee Kwan Yew warned of the importance of social stability and cooperation, "The essential conditions for industrialization will only be realized if there is close cooperation and understanding between Government, unions, and industrialists."[13]

In the interest of promoting labor stability and appearing more investment-friendly, the PAP government took action against the unions. For example, it passed legislation requiring union federations to register with the government, which could then de-register them for bad behavior, depriving the organizations of the legal right to exist. The government also took direct action against some militant leaders in the student and labor groups and even banished some from Singapore, as the Internal Security Act permitted for non-citizens. The restrictive actions and the PAP's procapitalist policies reignited the conflicts with the communist wing of the PAP that was still anticolonialist and anticapitalist. The conflict came to a head in 1961 when Lee Kwon Yew's tiger bared its fangs. The situation was so severe that in May the prime minister of the Malay Federation, Tenku Abdul Rahman, unexpectedly suggested in a speech that Singapore and the federation could move toward greater cooperation. The Malays had become so alarmed by the notion of a hostile, communist-controlled Singapore, should the PAP moderates lose control of the party, that having Singapore inside the federation, in some manner, suddenly seemed preferable to the alternative.

In July there was a special election in one of the voting districts. The communist wing of the PAP, led by Lim Chin Siong, together with some radical union leaders, supported the PAP challenger, David Marshall, now returned to politics as chair of the Workers' Party. Marshall won, running on a platform that advocated immediate independence from Britain, including the removal of the British from their military bases in Singapore as well as the elimination of the Internal Security Council. Lim Chin Siong advocated these positions, too, and opposed a merger with the anticommunists of the Malay Federation, dismissing the notion as continued imperialism.

These events unleashed a debate in the Legislative Assembly about Lee Kwan Yew's suitability to lead the country. In a narrow vote, 27 of the 51 assembly members voted in favor of the government.[14] The communist wing of the PAP responded by forming a new party, Barisan

Sosialis (BS) or Socialist Front. The new party was comprised of the members the PAP had pushed aside four years earlier, when they rewrote party policy to keep the extremists in the lower levels of the PAP. The defection to the BS, however, cost the PAP most of its lower-level organization and infrastructure that was in touch with the grass-roots, which caused another crisis for the party. Some supporters also fled anticipating that the PAP was simply going to implode. In the end, the PAP was left with too few seats in the Legislative Assembly to assure an affirmative vote if it could negotiate a merger with the federation.

THE MERGER

The tumult of the PAP crisis affirmed the federation's conclusion that if an acceptable approach could be found, merging with Singapore would be the safest course. Negotiations ensued with the issue of preserving Malay political power at the forefront of the agenda. As a compromise, leaders forged an agreement that would leave Singapore with disproportionately little representation in the federal government in exchange for considerably more local autonomy than other states in the federation. The BS spoke out in opposition and the PAP opted for a controversial referendum held in September 1962 to gauge public support. The public voted on the form of the merger but was not given a ballot option of voting against. The government plan received approval from 71 percent of the voters.[15] The British, who supported the merger, offered their holdings on the northern side of the nearby island of Borneo and this territory was then included in the merger plan.

In the interim, however, the BS was active in its resistance, and worked with opponents in the federation and in Borneo. With others, it sent a delegation to the United Nations to appeal to the Committee on Colonialism, against which Lee Kwan Yew himself went to New York to defend. The opposition was strongest in Brunei on Borneo, where Indonesia, which strongly opposed the merger, helped instigate resistance, and an armed revolt broke out in December 1962. The British military responded by inserting 2,000 troops in the space of only 60 hours, quickly putting down the rebellion.[16] The sultan of Brunei opted out of the merger agreement and planning went forward without Brunei.

However, proponents of the merger could not so quickly quell Indo-nesian opposition. Indonesia's interests rested in controlling all of the oil-rich island of Borneo, rather than only the portion that was already part of Indonesia. Sukarno also had a vision of uniting the Malay cultural space under his leadership. Finally, Sukarno worried about Singapore's ongoing prominence as a trading center, potentially strengthened further through merger, because it interfered with his economic nationalist policy of promoting trade through Indonesian ports.

In January 1963, Sukarno announced that he would not permit a merger to take place and launched a three-year undeclared war, known as *Konfrontasi* or Confrontation. He sent raiding parties into Borneo and Singapore, and up the Malay Peninsula. In Singapore, beginning in February, Indonesian fighter planes flew in formation as if to attack, forcing British Royal Air Force planes to scramble in response, though the Indonesians never followed through with an air attack. In the months and years that followed, however, the raiding parties targeted Singapore, attacking a petroleum installation and later setting off bombs. Security officials arrested more than 100 Indonesian operatives in Singapore on charges relating to the *Konfrontasi*. The Indonesian Navy also seized Singaporean fishing boats. The British, in charge of external security, responded with a show of force bringing in large reserves of ships, aircraft, and personnel to the bases in Singapore. Sukarno pointed to the military buildup as evidence that the federation was an imperial puppet.

The situation for the PAP and its political and organizational weakness changed just as the problems with Indonesia were starting. There is some disagreement among scholars as to whether the outcome was engineered by the PAP (the dominant viewpoint) or whether the PAP was simply the beneficiary of fortuitous circumstances outside of its control. Regardless of the interpretation, the Internal Security Council (comprised of three Britons, three Singaporeans, and a representative from the Malay Federation) took action against Singaporean communists in what is known as *Operation Cold Store* on the night of February 3, 1963. Security forces rounded up nearly 150 activists, among them journalists, students, labor unionists, and opposition politicians, who had allegedly supported the uprising in Brunei. They were detained without trial, and no charges were ever filed. The detainees included about half of the Executive Committee of the Barisan Sosialis, including Lim Chin Siong. Rioting by their supporters broke out after the security operation and more arrests followed, resulting in the jailing of many in the second tier of the BS organization. The BS was severely undercut, and the PAP was no longer burdened by BS competition.

The formal merger agreement was finalized in July 1963. The country's name would be Malaysia; and the federal government would be in charge of defense, internal security, and foreign affairs; but Singapore's local government had a high degree of autonomy over important areas like finance, education, and labor, as well as administrative authority for the day-to-day running of the island. The merger was to occur at the end of August, but then the Malay prime minister asked for a two-week delay due to issues with the *Konfrontasi*.

However, much to the surprise of the Malaysian leadership, Lee Kwan Yew went ahead and declared Singapore's independence from Britain two weeks ahead of the postponed merger date. In the interim, he called for immediate elections to confirm the PAP mandate for governing the new state in Malaysia. The PAP's strength was still compromised from having lost so much of the lower levels of the party organization to the BS, so the election outcome was not a foregone conclusion. However, the PAP did everything it could, within the limits of the law, to promote its success. Leaders called the election with the minimum amount of warning. Candidates had to present their documents in person, so the jailed BS members could not run. The government restricted some meetings, and froze union funds. The PAP also campaigned on its accomplishments of the previous four years. The government's Housing Development Board had constructed about as many housing units since 1960 as the prior housing agency had done in 30 years.[17] There were initiatives in health and immunization programs. The government had spent considerable funds on education and assured equality in the four-language school system. There were steps toward greater security, not just in tackling communist-incited unrest, but also secret societies. The government passed a Women's Charter, granting women greater security and legal rights. It had constructed dozens of community centers that provided people with a place for social interaction and space for programs like literacy classes and recreation. The community centers served as locations for publicizing PAP efforts and thus dovetailed with the campaign efforts. The new economic approach of import substitution, while it had not yet taken off (in fact, the Jurong industrial park had been nicknamed "Goh's Folly" after the Finance Minister Goh Keng Swee), was very much on the agenda. Finally, of course, the PAP could claim its greatest feat in having successfully negotiated merger with the Malay Federation.

Because of the district-based, winner-take-all election system borrowed from Britain (similar to that used in the United States House of Representatives), the PAP only won 47 percent of the vote, but 37 of the 51 seats (or 74%).[18] However, success came at a cost. The Malay leaders in Kuala Lumpur were not pleased with the premature declaration of independence or the hastily called election. The merger went forward in mid-September as planned but with an added touch of bitterness in this marriage of convenience between Singapore and Malaysia.

ONWARD TO THE REPUBLIC OF SINGAPORE

Lee Kwan Yew's actions in the final weeks before merger contributed to an already established tension in the relationship with Malay officials. Since Singapore was to retain a significant degree of financial autonomy, the PAP negotiated for beneficial financial arrangements in the merger agreement. The party got what it wanted, but its negotiating partners felt it had pushed too hard and insisted on taking too much. This started the merger off on a bad foot and it soon worsened from there.

In April 1964, national elections were scheduled in Malaysia. Lee Kwan Yew agreed in a sort of gentleman's agreement to sit out the election and not compete on the national level until the next election. However, Lee Kwan Yew became concerned that Malaysian Chinese would shift their support from the Malay Chinese Association (MCA) to the BS, which opposed merger, and that the merger effort would thereby be undermined. Despite the fact that the MCA was allied with the Prime Minister Tunku's United Malays National Organization, the PAP entered the election in opposition to the MCA. UMNO leaders saw this as a breach of the agreement between Lee Kwan Yew and Tunku. There was backlash from people fearing the PAP, from predominantly Chinese Singapore, was trying to assert itself too much into Malay-dominated politics, and Tunku publicly reaffirmed his alliance with the MCA and against the PAP. The PAP won only a single seat outside Singapore,[19] which confirmed the poor reception of the PAP's actions.

The next blow to merger was two five-day episodes of rioting in Singapore between the Chinese and Malay communities, the first in July and the second in September 1964. It was the worst and longest rioting in Singapore since World War II. The Malays were angry that the special provisions for Malays in the other parts of Malaysia, such as the quota system in the civil service, were not to be applied in Singapore. Lee Kwan Yew instead spoke for equality of opportunity across all the ethnic groups. A meeting between representatives from the Malay community and Lee Kwan Yew corresponded to a planned event honoring the birthday of the Prophet Muhammad. Fighting broke out between Malay attendees and Chinese hecklers. By the time police restored order, 22 were dead and 454 injured. The murder of a Malay bicycle-rickshaw driver sparked the second wave of riots. In that episode, 12 were killed, 109 injured, and more than 1200 arrested for disorderly conduct or curfew violations.[20] Motivated by the tensions caused by the riots, the Indonesians staged further raids in Singapore and in the rest of Malaysia to push the conflict ever higher. In other parts of Malaysia, these events confirmed the perceived anti-Muslim bias on the part of the Chinese, and there was fear the ethnic conflict could spread.

The general PAP attitude toward Malay policies of development and communal relations was also a stumbling block and proved an impossible gap to bridge. As exemplified by the Malay quota system, the Malay political system was built on protecting Malay political power from Chinese influence, since the Chinese had disproportionate economic power. Singaporean politics were about communal inclusion rather than division. The policies for economic and social development also reflected the differing approaches. Singapore advocated for maintaining its free-port policy, while Malaysia wanted trade barriers. As a decision-deferring compromise, they decided on a 12-year period to introduce a common market between the two territorial units. The PAP advocated well-being for all citizens coming from economic progress with socialist-style programs to spread the wealth. The Malay leadership consisted of conservative Malay aristocrats; Tunku was a prince, son of a sultan. They wanted to protect their status and allied with elite Malay Chinese who had little interest in sharing their wealth with the masses. Vastly different and incompatible ideologies shaped the two sets of political elites. Lee Kwan Yew spoke of Malaysia's "feudal" politics and argued strongly and publicly for approaches conforming to PAP ideas. He wanted to address the problems dividing the societies head on, whereas Tunku and his UMNO colleagues felt the divisions were so deep that only time could bridge societal schisms.

The various problems, including ideological incompatibility, concerns about excessive Chinese influence and inadequate Chinese respect for Malay culture, a lack of trust between the two sets of leaders, and the tensions from the Indonesian *Konfrontasi* combined to make the situation intolerable for Malay elites. Lee Kwan Yew, who saw himself as above ethnic politics but was the personification of the Chinese threat in the minds of the Malays, became the target for the worry and dislike. The UMNO elite debated the best way to handle the situation and concluded that either the PAP's leadership of Singapore or Singapore itself had to go. Believing that it would be difficult to remove the PAP from Singapore's government, the Malay leaders decided Singapore needed to leave Malaysia. Negotiations between the two parties led to Singapore's announcement of its independence on August 9, 1965. Various Commonwealth members, including Britain and Australia, as well as the United States immediately recognized Singapore as an independent country. In September, the United Nations admitted it for membership. The Republic of Singapore had launched.

The post-war period was a tumultuous time. The difficulties of rebuilding the infrastructure and economy, as well as restoring social trust and order challenged colonial leaders. Then new, radical political forces arose and pushed the country away from Britain on its own distinctive path, with and without Malaysia. All of this happened in an environment shaped by competition between leading ideologies spread around the world through globalization. The struggle between capitalism and communism acutely shaped Singapore's history during this time.

NOTES

1. C. M. Turnbull, *A History of Singapore, 1819–1988*, 2nd ed. (New York, NY: Oxford University Press, 1989), 220.

2. John Springhall, "Mountbattan versus the Generals: British Military Rule in Singapore, 1945-46," *Journal of Contemporary History* 36 (2001), 643.

3. Ibid., 647.

4. C. M. Turnbull, *A History of Singapore*, 228.

5. Ibid, 235.

6. Carl A. Trocki, *Singapore: Wealth, Power and the Culture of Control* (New York, NY: Routledge, 2006), 117.

7. C. M. Turnbull, *A History of Singapore*, 252.

8. Ibid., 256.

9. Ibid., 258.

10. Carl A. Trocki, *Singapore: Wealth, Power and the Culture of Control*, 161–162.

11. Emma Sadka, "Singapore and the Federation: Problems of Merger," *Asian Survey* 1 (1962), 23.

12. Ibid, 18, 20.

13. Quoted in Carl A. Trocki, *Singapore: Wealth, Power and the Culture of Control*, 122.

14. C. M. Turnbull, *A History of Singapore*, 271–272.

15. Ibid., 273.

16. Malcolm Murfett et al., *Between Two Oceans* (New York: Marshall Cavendish International, 2004), 386–387.

17. C. M. Turnbull, *A History of Singapore*, 276.

18. Ibid., 277.

19. Carl A. Trocki, *Singapore: Wealth, Power and the Culture of Control*, 126.

20. Lay Yuen Tan, "Communal riots of 1964," Singapore National Library, http://infopedia.nl.sg/articles/SIP_45_2005-01-06.html.

7

From Third World to First World: Since 1965

Since its independence in 1965, Singapore's transformation has astonished observers around the globe. The degree of progress in economic and social development, and the speed of change, is nearly unrivaled. After the merger with Malaysia failed, Singapore had little to recommend it other than an excellent location and a hardworking population. It had little land, no natural resources, an economy that was vulnerable to fluctuations in international trade, and an economic development program that was unviable. The obstacles before the political leadership, the People's Action Party (PAP), were immense, but they successfully charted a new course for Singapore. The focus of their efforts was forward thinking: they were at the leading edge of poor countries using export-oriented manufacturing for economic development, essentially a step into contemporary economic globalization. Along with Hong Kong, South Korea, and Taiwan, Singapore became part of the elite group known as the Four Asian Tigers, newly industrializing economies with some of the highest economic growth rates in the world. Across the decades, the government shifted strategies to stay with, or ahead of, the global economic trendsetters, and it has paid off. In terms of social development, the government pursued policies that improved the quality of life for many people, especially in the areas of housing, education, and health. The area that has made the least progress is political development toward a free and democratic government; the government holds regular elections but limits basic freedoms of press, speech and assembly, and suppresses political opposition before it can develop into a competitive force. Thus, while the economic benefits have been enormous, Singapore's development has not come without cost, at least to some individuals.

THE EARLY YEARS OF INDEPENDENCE, 1965–1973

Prior to ejection from the federation with Malaysia, the PAP set a course, under the advisement of the World Bank, toward import-substitution industrialization, which was a typical approach at the time for developing countries. Under this type of industrial development, countries erect considerable trade barriers against imports from other countries and seek to develop domestic industries to produce and replace goods that were once imported. The government hoped these industries, mostly low-wage and labor intensive, such as textiles, would absorb many of the unemployed workers (10% in 1960[1]). Success in import substitution depended, in part, on a domestic market that was large enough to purchase the new domestic products. While there was a large potential market for domestic products when Singapore was part of Malaysia, Singapore's population of just less than two million was not adequate for a successful domestic market. Thus, upon independence, the political leadership immediately shifted to a different strategy.

Economic Development

The PAP pursued export-led industrialization that would be funded primarily through foreign investments. This was necessary for several reasons. Hong Kong and Taiwan had benefited from the flight of industrial entrepreneurs from the People's Republic of China, whereas Singapore had commercial entrepreneurs but few with industrial experience. Moreover, Singapore could not rely on regional trade or investment because of trade barriers in the neighboring countries. Finally, due to a political climate created in the 1950s, the political leadership had the opportunity to focus on foreign funding. In the 1950s, the PAP embraced the left-leaning masses of poor laborers as the party's base. The wealthy conservatives were sidelined by the over-whelming electoral strength of the PAP and lost political status within society. This left the PAP free to pursue whatever policies it wished, without feeling the political pressure to take wealthy domestic inter-ests into account. The PAP chose to focus almost exclusively on what foreign investors would offer, which, in addition to funding, was also managerial expertise and ready markets for the exported goods.

To create an inviting foreign investment climate, the government put a number of policies into place. First, it implemented a series of financial incentives, including substantial tax breaks. Second, the government positioned itself as a low-risk investment environment through peaceful labor relations. To prevent the labor unrest that had plagued Singapore in the decade before independence, the government passed legislation intended to limit conflict and improve productivity, including limited vacation time, longer working hours, and reduced payments for overtime. Decisions relating to job assign-ments, promotions, lay-offs, etc. were placed solely in the hands of management and were no longer subject to negotiation, which had been a prior source of labor-management conflict. Concessions to workers included sick leave, severance pay for lay-offs, and increased employer contributions to the national retirement fund, the Central Provident Fund. In 1971, the government took a further step with the creation of the National Wages Council, on which members from the government, labor, and management worked together to set wage levels. Collectively these policies created a very stable work environ-ment, which, coupled with government programs for vocational and technical training to provide basic skills to the workforce, made Singapore a desirable investment locale.

While working on the foundations of this favorable investment environment, the government acted in other ways to advance the export-led growth plan. It revamped the Economic Development Board, created shortly before independence. It continued to promote economic development but shifted financing operations to the new Development Bank of Singapore. The Development Bank provided funding partnerships to private capital investments, particularly if an investor was wary of funding a project alone, giving government-related institutions a considerable role in the development of Singapore's economy. In addition to providing funding, the government established a number of government-led companies, many of which formed joint-venture partnerships with foreign corporations. These government-led companies are an enduring feature of Singapore's government-managed economy. This affiliation with the government has lent them credibility and security as partners for investors, but they nevertheless function largely as independent, for-profit, competitive companies. The government quickly formed government-led companies in areas that it especially wanted to target for growth, including transport, shipbuilding, oil refining, and more. By 1974, the government had some involvement in at least 124 different companies.[2]

While forming these plans, the government suffered a blow that threatened its progress. In 1968, the British government announced that it would withdraw from its naval and army bases in Singapore within three years. This raised a number of security concerns, but it also would have a negative economic impact. British military spending accounted for 20 percent of Singapore's revenue at the time[3] and for tens of thousands of jobs.[4] The immediate fear was a sharp increase in unemployment. Lee Kwan Yew traveled to London to explain Singapore's position and won a number of concessions from the British. Singapore's government gained control of all military facilities, including schools, hospitals, shipyards, airfields, and 10 percent of the land on the island in addition to assistance with job retraining, a defense system, and a sizable financial award. What initially looked like potential disaster was turned into lucrative opportunities through the exploitation of these new resources. For example, the Sembawang Naval Base became a major port installation and was central in Singapore's development of shipbuilding and ship repair industries.

The new resources left Singapore well positioned to capitalize on several international economic developments of the time. There was increasing oil exploration in Southeast Asia and Singapore's existing port, petroleum storage facilities, and small refining infrastructure, as well as its location between Middle Eastern oil suppliers and top users in Asia, left it well positioned to become the region's petroleum center. Already in the 1960s, Mobil set up operations in Singapore to service its Indonesian oil fields, and in 1970 Esso opened a refinery. Seeking to promote itself in this arena, the government established the Singapore Refining Company to develop joint ventures with foreign companies. The high quality facilities at the Sembawang port were useful in these endeavors, particularly for shipping, storage, and supporting oil exploration operations. The involvement of the United States in the war in Vietnam created demand for petroleum and other products, and helped drive the boom that Singapore experienced during this time. By 1970, oil comprised 40 percent of Singapore's manufactured exports,[5] and within a few years, it was one of the world's top refining centers.

Concerns about transiting the Suez Canal because of conflict between Israel and its Arab neighbors increased demand for shipping support in Asia. Singapore quickly established the goal of becoming the second biggest shipping, shipbuilding, and ship repair site in Asia, behind Japan. The effects of these efforts were immediate: The revenue from Singapore's shipbuilding and repair nearly doubled in just two years, from $64 million in 1966 to $120 million in 1968.[6] The Sembawang shipyard was eventually an asset for that undertaking. To offer further support for the project, the government established another government-led company, the Neptune Orient Line. Improving existing port facilities, including a major expansion of container shipping capacity completed in the early 1970s, also added to the success.

Regional trade also increased after the first few years of independence. The *Konfrontasi* conflict ended in 1966, improving relations with Indonesia. Tensions remained with Malaysia, but Singapore began trying to repair these relations. In 1970, Singapore offered local entrepreneurs a tax benefit to invest in Malaysia and Indonesia. A short time later Lee Kwan Yew made his first Malaysian visit since the failed merger, resulting in the division of several joint Singaporean-Malaysian economic ventures that had caused ongoing tensions between the two countries. For example, the joint airline, Malaysia-Singapore Airlines, was decoupled and two separate airlines were established; Singapore Airlines, a government-owned corporation, subsequently became one of the world's most highly regarded air carriers. These reduced tensions with both Malaysia and Indonesia opened the door to increased regional trade, which further helped Singapore's growth.

Another major development was the decision of Bank of America to establish a "dollar market" in Singapore. The goal was to make U.S. dollars available for loans to borrowers in the region. The government successfully courted Bank of America to make Singapore the site of this market by offering a range of tax incentives, such as exempting from taxation the interest earnings of foreign depositors. Other banks soon followed Bank of America's example in establishing financial operations, including a gold market, in Singapore. These activities created a sizable financial sector that provided diversity in Singapore's economy, making it less vulnerable to shifting economic trends associated with a narrower economic base.

Singapore's economy changed dramatically during this era, with an average economic growth rate of 10 percent in the 1960s and accelerating even faster in the 1970s.[7] Until the new economic program was put into place, 70 percent of Singapore's foreign investment came from

Britain.[8] Soon, however, that shifted as funds flowed from the United States, other European countries, Hong Kong, Taiwan, Malaysia, and Australia. By 1972, the United States was the source of 46 percent of foreign investment and the following year became the biggest trading partner next to Malaysia. Moreover, 70 percent of the value of manufactured goods was produced by companies that were partly or entirely foreign owned and these goods comprised 83 percent of exports, shifting much of Singapore's trade away from entrepôt commerce.[9] In terms of percentages of gross domestic product (GDP), in 1965 commerce accounted for 30 percent and manufacturing 15 percent. By 1973, commerce had dropped to 26 percent and manufacturing rose to 24 percent of GDP.[10] The government succeeded at reducing unemployment to such a degree that, by the early 1970s, Singapore had to import foreign workers to meet demand for labor.

Social Development

Accompanying the economic progress were significant improvements in social development. At the time of independence, Singapore, like many poor countries, was plagued by substandard housing, housing shortages, health problems, and an undereducated population. The government sought to rectify the problems. While the PAP advocated socialism, it is important to note that this was not a form of socialism that would be recognizable in a Western context. In the West, socialism implies a welfare state with a range of government programs to assist the poor and needy, in particular, but generally to redistribute wealth and minimize income inequalities. Often these efforts will take the form of government-funded health care programs, government-funded pensions, subsidized housing and food assistance for poorer people, financial support for the disabled and unemployed, and sometimes even government-assisted daycare and elder care. In its most comprehensive form, the government may offer "cradle to grave" assistance to its citizens. Singapore's approach was (and continues to be) quite different. In fact, the government viewed the welfare state as undermining both the work ethic of citizens and the family as the basic unit of society, which bears responsibility for the wellbeing of all family members. The government made social investments that would support economic growth.

One of the government's first acts was to expand the Central Provident Fund, the retirement savings system, from applying only to government employees to applying to all employees, a system that still exists today. Unlike in an American-style social security program, the government's role is small and there is no redistribution of wealth. Workers and employers are both required to pay a certain percentage, initially 25 percent for each party, into a savings fund from which workers can later draw. This was a major step for providing for the long-term wellbeing of Singaporeans.

Hand-in-hand with the Central Provident Fund was the work of the Housing Development Board. Initially it built thousands of high-rise apartment for lower-income Singaporeans; with time, it expanded into building somewhat larger apartments for middle-income citizens. The scale and scope of construction was enormous as whole new towns were created, the first, Queenstown, as early as the mid-1960s and the second new town by 1973. These towns sought to meet all needs: People could work, shop, obtain healthcare, and enjoy other services all within the created town, and they had access to the growing public transit system when they needed to leave the new town. This removed people from the slum-like conditions of the dense urban center, and allowed the government to gain control of that land, replacing old dwellings and shops with office and hotel skyscrapers to support new business development. While the Housing Development Board constructed and operated many of the apartment buildings, the model was not one of pure social support. There was some subsidy given, but overall the residents paid the costs. The savings in the Central Provident Fund assisted the government in financing the housing construction as well as improvements to the infrastructure, including basic utilities, roads, and public transit.

This large-scale housing construction had significant social implications relating to Singapore's ethnic composition. The official policy of the new country was multiculturalism. The four school systems in each language had legal equality, and any of the four languages could be used in the parliament. The government granted official recognition to holidays from each religious group (two Hindu, two Muslim, and one Chinese), although it was left to the individual communities to sponsor celebrations as the government remained a neutral actor above the fray of ethnic difference. While government officials spoke out in support of Chinese-medium schools, any hint of advocacy for one ethnic group was condemned as ethnic chauvinism, which was incompatible with the goal of a multicultural society. Indeed, the government's policy was that ethnic conflict could destroy the state, so the wellbeing and, indeed, the survival of the country depended on ethnic harmony. In this context, the work of the Housing Development Board led to massive social integration. The old ethnic enclaves were razed and citizens from all over Singapore were relocated into ethnically mixed apartment complexes. One of the government's tasks was to forge a Singaporean national identity that transcended ethnic difference, and creating ethnically integrated living spaces was a central feature in the project.

Another major social construction project involved education, which needed to be transformed to accommodate the demands of the developing economy. In 1966, the government introduced bilingualism into the schools whereby students would study one of the other four languages in addition to the language of instruction in their school. The schools developed a special emphasis on marketable skills that could be used in the industries, with particular focus on technology and science. Since English was seen as the language of commerce and technology, many parents opted for English education. The schools were also an important tool for national identity formation. For example, since 1966, students recite the National Pledge, "We, the citizens of Singapore, pledge ourselves as one united people, regardless of race, language or religion, to build a democratic society, based on justice and equality so as to achieve happiness, prosperity and progress for our nation," at school assemblies and on important national days.

The goal of improving quality of life also necessitated changes in health care. The government launched a program of immunizations to combat diseases like smallpox and polio. Land reclamation projects, involving drainage programs, increased useable land for both housing and industrial development while helping with mosquito-borne illnesses like malaria. The expansion of the infrastructure gave nearly everyone access to piped water, and connection to the sewer system, which helped control illnesses from contaminated water, like cholera. These efforts improved the overall health of the people and soon the leading killers mirrored those of wealthy countries: heart disease and cancer instead of preventable diseases.

The last major social development issue the government tackled in the early years was problematically high population growth, which worsened the problem of unemployment. The Singapore Family Planning and Population Board was established in 1966, and charged with leading the effort to achieve zero population growth. The Board launched a Stop at Two campaign, encouraging people to have no more than two children, and the government established penalties and incentives to encourage compliance. Families with more than two children were placed lower on the priority list for government-built housing; government employees who had more than two children were denied maternity leave; hospitals charged higher fees for delivering the third and successive children; and no tax deductions were given for any children beyond the second. Simultaneously, the government legalized abortion and voluntary sterilization. The program, coming at the same time as increasing education and improved job prospects for women as well as increasing wealth (all demographic shifts associated with reduced population growth), worked almost immediately.

Political Development

One might expect that independence would come with a certain amount of political change. In fact, there was very little. The Legislative Assembly became the Parliament and an appointed president took on the ceremonial role of head of state. Otherwise, the constitutional structures remained unchanged from those established in the late 1950s. The PAP's unfettered control of government remained intact, enabling the party to initiate the economic and social development programs. While the party won a majority of seats in both 1959 and 1963, developments in 1966 cemented its hold on power. The opposition party, Barisan Sosialis (BS), sorely undermined by previous security actions that resulted in the imprisonment of much of its leadership, opposed the newly independent state, claiming it was a neocolonial entity, and BS members of parliament boycotted the parliamentary sessions. In 1965 and in 1966, the BS tried to mobilize student protests at Nanyang University. The University expelled students both times, and added the requirement of a voucher attesting to "suitability" for university admission. Security officials jailed more party members. Through 1966, the BS members of parliament gradually resigned and, by the end, the PAP controlled all of the parliamentary seats. In the 1968 elections, the PAP won all the seats, although there were only a handful of voting districts where opposing candidates ran for election. In 1972, there were contests for most of the seats, and the overall PAP vote declined to 70 percent,[11] but it still managed to sweep the election and control all seats in Parliament.

It appears that the PAP leaders' early struggles, particularly against the political unrest and threat from its own communist wing as well as problems with ethnic rioting in Singapore and Malaysia, left the leaders with a jaundiced eye toward democracy. They viewed it as a tool of communists and those advocating ethnic divisions. The leaders' own comments make their position plain: Lee Kwan Yew said, "...checks and balances interfere with governing in a developing country where executive action must be swift,"[12] and that one could not "...allow subversives to get away by insisting that I [have] got to prove everything against them in a court of law."[13] Kishore Mahbubani, Deputy Secretary for Foreign Affairs, wrote,

> "Freedom does not only solve problems; it can also create them.
> The United States has undertaken a massive social experiment,
> tearing down social institution after social institution that con-
> strained the individual. The results have been disastrous. . . .
> Many a society shudders at the prospects of this happening
> on its shores. But instead of traveling overseas with humility,
> Americans confidently preach the virtues of unfettered individ-
> ual freedom, blithely ignoring the visible social consequences."[14]
> Another PAP leader expressed it this way, ". . . I don't believe
> that consultation with the people is a very productive exercise.
> People, even with education, tend to be irrational."[15]

With that rhetoric in the background, charges of weak democracy, and even human rights abuses, have plagued Singapore virtually since its founding. The government justifies its actions and positions in several ways. First, PAP leaders argue that good government provides for the wellbeing of its citizens and, thus, anything that potentially undermines Singapore's desirability as a global center for investment, trade, finance, etc. must be stopped. This includes anything that could compromise Singapore's political stability such as political unrest or ethnic conflict. Democracy, in their view, invites both those risks and must, therefore, be limited. Second, the PAP is quick to point out that in their regular elections, in which people are free to express their political preferences, voters return the PAP to leadership in election after election. Finally, the PAP argues cultural difference: Unlike in individualist Western societies, Asian societies like Singapore put the interests of the group first, and that it is both unfair and culturally imperialist to place Western, individualist demands on a society that made different cultural choices. The argument that trumps all, however, is economic: If it is good for the economy, it is good for Singapore, and political stability via the PAP is good for the economy.

The PAP achieved its exclusive hold on political authority by suppressing potential opponents, and controlling society. It is important to recognize in this context that there was no practical difference between the PAP and the government. Many scholars look to the demise of independent community organizations as a major tool of PAP control, as organizations unaffiliated with the PAP have been co-opted, intimidated, or driven out of existence by the PAP. The Chinese community, for example, had a vibrant network of clan, regional, temple, and burial-society organizations that thrived throughout the colonial period. Many of these organizations revolved around the leaders in the Singapore Chinese Chamber of Commerce, who were elites by virtue of the individual wealth they had amassed. However, the PAP's need for loyalty for social stability led it to undermine any organization that could compete for people's loyalty, and the organizations of the Chinese community fell on hard times after independence. The government especially tightened restrictions on activities by ethnic communal groups after ethnic rioting in Malaysia in 1969. Student groups, known for their political activism, also faced restrictions. Students at the University of Singapore were not permitted to select their own student union officers, and the university administration controlled the union's funding. More intimidating for students, however, was likely the knowledge that the PAP influenced many hiring decisions for both government jobs and those in government-related companies. Anyone marked as a troublemaker was unlikely to find a good job after finishing college. It was government regulations that undermined the labor unions, in the course of their consolidation into the progovernment National Trades Union Congress, and also through the loss of most of their functions with the labor and wage regulations that the government implemented as part of its economic development plan.

In lieu of unaffiliated community organizations, the government created a network of new ones. Already in 1960, the government established the People's Association, which was charged with running community centers, kindergartens, and other amenities to increase social connectedness. Many of these were launched along with the new apartment complexes being built to help create a new sense of community as people moved from their old neighborhoods. However, the organizations were also tools of social control. For example, in order to teach kindergarten, one had to be a PAP member, and government-trained staff operated the community centers. The People's Association also served as an umbrella for a number of Citizens' Consultative Committees, which were supposed to be independent of the party but did not develop in that manner. The name implies they would be a vehicle for citizen input and feedback but instead are a downward communication avenue from government to people.

The government also extended its political authority through media control. The broadcast media had been in government hands since the beginning. The print media, in contrast, had historically been an instrument of communist provocation, prompting the government to exert stricter authority. In 1971, the government targeted newspapers, and by the end of the year, only one of four English-language newspapers, the *Straits Times*, still existed. Simultaneously, the government challenged the non-English newspapers by suggesting they were foreign influenced, which threatened national security, and targeted journalists who worked for those papers.

Several colonial-era control laws were repeatedly renewed in case efforts at co-opting or intimidating opponents failed, specifically the Internal Security Act and the Preservation of Public Security Ordinance, both of which permit detention without trial. Both of these measures had a pre-independence track record of effectiveness, making their retention desirable. For example, the Internal Security Act had been used as part of *Operation Cold Store* in 1963, through which PAP leader and communist organizer Lim Chin Siong was jailed for six years. The Preservation of Public Security Ordinance had been used against the *Straits Times* in 1959 when its journalists were threatened with arrest and detention for questioning the merger with Malaysia. These laws were further expanded to assure social control into Singapore's years of independence.

While establishing and maintaining authority was a primary task for the PAP in the early years, another project, developing political culture, also received due attention. One aspect of the political culture formation was tied to the multicultural national identity discussed above, but there were other important characteristics of the emergent political culture that affected Singapore's political, social, and economic development. In a sense, the values promoted by the PAP were a blurring of the lines between the economic and the political, with emphasis on meritocracy, integrity, competition, efficiency, discipline, self-reliance, and respect for success.

These values applied to government and policy in a variety of ways. The government emphasized merit in its decisions on education policy, such as linking academic performance to admission and scholarships for college, as opposed to considering social concerns like ethnic representation for admission decisions or financial need for scholarships. Academic performance was also the basis for employment after graduation rather than non-merit-based factors like personal connections. The education system featured a tracking system so top-performing students, even at elementary levels, could be directed into successively more elite paths. Encouragement of self-reliance was evident in the decisions regarding a welfare state with, for example, pension funds being established as workers' savings plans, rather than a government-supported program. These values even shaped PAP candidate selection. PAP officials had to pass a screening process before being allowed to run for office. Many were headhunted based on strong performance in the bureaucracy, government-led corporations, or the private sector. If individuals did not perform up to the level of party expectation, they were dismissed. Integrity is obvious in the almost corruption-free governance that leaders considered important for attracting investment to Singapore. In many ways, the state, society, and economy blended for the common cause of economic growth.

In addition to facing domestic challenges, the leaders of the new country had foreign policy concerns to address. Foreign Minister Sinnathamby Rajaratnam, who held the post from independence until 1980, was widely considered a master diplomat. He recognized Singapore's dependence on relationships with other countries for economic wellbeing and national security. The improved relations with Indonesia and Malaysia that opened the door to trade also facilitated diplomatic relationships. Rajaratnam was crucial to Singapore's inclusion among the founding members (together with Indonesia, Malaysia, Philippines, and Thailand) of the Association of Southeast Asian Nations (ASEAN), an important step in Singapore's political globalization. ASEAN members worked together for mutual economic development and regional security, including combating narcotics trafficking and policing the Strait of Melaka, which continued to have problems with piracy. Singapore's government, however, recognized the global power of the United States as an important piece of Singapore's security configuration, particularly once the British completed their military withdrawal from Singapore. Immediately after independence, the country implemented a policy creating a military and compulsory national service for most Singaporean males; however in the case of a broader conflict, Singapore recognized the need for bigger, more powerful allies. In the early years, leaders reached out to Israel for military training and advice, as Israel used the military to integrate members of a diverse society, and could thus serve as a model for Singapore. The Israeli military also had experience in defending itself against much larger and stronger neighbors, something Singapore initially feared it might need to do. Relations with Israel also indirectly aligned Singapore with the United States. The military relationship with Israel ended once relations with Malaysia and Indonesia improved, but it serves as an example of both the breadth and strategic nature of Singapore's foreign relations, not just for trade but for security and diplomacy.

Singapore's first years as a country recorded amazing levels of development. A World Bank/International Monetary Fund report from 1970 painted a picture of success, saying that Singapore had "a general sense of ebullience & optimism" and "it is this proper sense of urgency which makes Singapore such an exciting place to live in and which, tempered as it is with humanity & concern for the well-being of the individual citizen, lies at the heart of Singapore's outstandingly successful development & achievements."[16] More critical evaluators point to the price of democracy and justice. In the words of Lee Kwan Yew, "I am often accused of interfering in the private lives of citizens. Ye[t], if I did not . . . we wouldn't be here today. And I say without the slightest remorse, that we wouldn't be here, we would not have made economic progress, if we had not intervened on very personal matters–who your neighbor is, how you live, the noise you make, how you spit, or what language you use. We decide what's right. Never mind what the people think."[17]

ONGOING GROWTH, 1973–1990

While Singapore's accomplishments were considerable, the government was careful not to slow down and fall behind the curve. Much of the world experienced a severe economic downturn in 1973–1974, but Singapore weathered it well thanks to a diversified economy and massive government spending on housing, infrastructure, etc. However, leaders saw the need for changes in the economic development strategy and the need for social progress and political action to support those endeavors.

New Economic Development Plans

The initial economic plan solved the problem of unemployment by creating many low-skill, low-wage jobs but a problem that had grown worse was income inequality. Lee Kwan Yew acknowledged that development had been substantial but not just or equal. By the early 1970s, the per capita income was the second highest in Asia. Singapore had a small group of extremely wealthy people, but the common worker had been left behind, with worker wages rising only about 5 percent compared to a 100–200 percent increase in executive compensation.[18] In order to address this disparity, the government developed a new economic plan that invited higher skill, and thus higher paying and higher profit, jobs to replace the low-paying, sweatshop-type jobs created by the initial wave of industrialization.

Leaders announced a program, ultimately nicknamed the second industrial revolution, to replace labor-intensive work with technology-intensive work. The National Wages Council implemented "corrective wage policy" in which it increased wages to levels competitive for medium- to high-tech industries, thereby forcing man-ufacturers either to upgrade their production to merit higher wages or move their low-skill work to another country. The government increased training programs, gave tax breaks for training expenses related to medium- and high-tech employment, and gave more tax breaks to companies in desired industries to new establish operations in Singapore or to upgrade existing ones. Initially, certain high-skill foreign workers, such as engineers, were admitted to jumpstart the development. The targeted industries included petrochemicals, preci-sion engineering, aerospace, electronics, computer software and hard-ware, medical instruments, office equipment, etc.

The petrochemical focus was logical given the ongoing importance of the oil industry, including exploration, extraction, and refining. In the 1970s, extensive new oil fields were found in the Gulf of Thailand, the Indonesian archipelago, and the South China Sea; Malaysia, Thailand, Philippines, and Vietnam became oil-producing countries, but Singapore had the advantage with an already well-established infrastructure. From 1977 to 1982, 40 percent of Singapore's gross manufacturing exports was oil,[19] although that percentage soon decreased as the new industrial pro-gram increased exports in other areas, especially electronics. The govern-ment's commitment to the new industries was vast: To provide space for large petrochemical factories, it undertook land reclamation, and one, large Jurong Island emerged from seven small islands.

Massive amounts of new foreign investment flowed in, doubling between 1979 and 1984.[20] In addition to the new industries, increases in off-shore banking caused growth in the banking sector, and height-ened Singapore's prominence as a financial center. All of this helped further diversify the economy, which became an increasing priority for the government to assure continued, steady growth. The Economic Development Board increased its promotional efforts by opening 22 offices in the United States, Japan, and Europe, all of which had been targets for luring investment since the beginning. The Economic Development Board could highlight many desirable characteristics in its marketing. Singapore offered skilled and English-speaking work-ers; a highly improved infrastructure with quality communications facilities, expanded and mechanized port facilities, and a new international airport at Changi; a taxation and regulatory system that favored business; and political stability and noncorrupt government that facilitated the security of investments. Changes in the economic policies of China also yielded new economic opportunities; as China opened its markets, Singapore, with its large ethnic Chinese popula-tion, positioned itself to capitalize on the situation.

However, the mid-1980s brought Singapore's first economic down-turn since independence with a drop in per capita income and gross domestic product. The recession especially affected manufacturing and oil refining. This was a surprising event as people had become accustomed to growth, and there was talk of malaise and charges that Singaporeans were insufficiently entrepreneurial. A special taskforce concluded that the recession was caused by changes in the global economy and that Singapore's international competitiveness was declining. The government implemented a series of new priorities and plans to turn things around. To reduce business expenses and help Singapore become a center for profitability again, policy makers cut business taxes, utility costs, international telephone charges, and employer contributions to the Central Provident Fund, and the government offered subsidies for property rentals and port fees. The government also pushed for advanced technology and higher value-added business investments. The focus shifted to marketing Singapore as a "total business center" for international corporations where Singapore could serve as a regional company headquarters with proximity to production sites in nearby countries that had cheaper labor costs. Singapore could offer a range of business support services like banking, accounting, and law along with motivated and experienced managers. Again the government initiated new programs to increase the skills and productivity of the workforce, with special training for clerical, administrative, and technical staff. The strategy was successful: by 1991, 3,000 international corporations had Singapore-based offices, including Citibank, DuPont, General Electric, Hewlett-Packard, and IBM.[21]

A second strategy attempted to capitalize on Singapore's many small- and medium-sized companies, many of which were Chinese family firms that had been virtually ignored in the government's development plans up to that point. The government hoped these firms could exploit China's entry into globalization by establishing trade rela-tionships, finding investment opportunities, and meeting the demands of China's growing wealthy elite. This was part of Singapore's plan to become an international investor in the surrounding region, rather than just a recipient of international investment. The government-led corpo-rations partnered with the small- and medium-sized companies for much of this activity. Economic planners also hoped that Singapore, with its total business center assets, could employ its Chinese-speaking population as an intermediary for European and American companies that lacked the language skills and cultural insights for easy business relationships in China.

Societal Shifts

Many social changes happened during the first years after Singapore's independence, but the government's social engineering programs continued. Two programs seem connected to the ongoing development of a national identity. While government rhetoric touted multiculturalism, a communal slant developed through the creation of pro-Chinese programs. Government leaders, including Lee Kwan Yew (who once said of himself, "I am no more Chinese than President Kennedy was an Irishman"[22]), promoted Chinese-language education, suggesting that English-educated Singaporeans lacked cultural roots. To combat this perceived problem, one program promoted what leaders called Confucian Values, specifically traditional Chinese values, such as discipline, industriousness, frugality, family-orientation, etc. Administrators added Confucian and other Asian values courses to school curricula. While it may have been aimed at forming identity and creating roots, some scholars have pointed out that Confucian values also support a hierarchical society where benevolent leaders rule at will and elites are not challenged, which would support a government's control of society and economy. Around this time, too, the government drastically cut social programs, such as financial support for people with disabilities, since it was a family's responsibility to take care of people who needed assistance, and everyone who could possibly work should do so. The other program advocated the use of Mandarin by everyone, from food hawkers to business executives. Speaking Mandarin could not only be used to do business with China but also to promote economic relations with Taiwan and give Singapore an edge over Westerners and the Cantonese-speaking people of Hong Kong. The campaign was also an attempt to unify the Chinese community and to undermine the ongoing use of dialects. The bottom line was that the government wanted people to speak proper Chinese, and that was Mandarin.

Beyond government initiatives, results of the efforts to build a multicultural identity seemed mixed at most. Intermarriage rates among communities remained low, even when there were no religious differences. The Malay ethnic group showed signs of difficulties, particularly as the government gradually removed the few special provisions they had as a group (such as free college tuition). While there were some poor Chinese, the Malay group more than others lagged in socioeconomic progress, such as wealth and educational attainment. In 1981, the government set aside funding for the establishment of a Malay community organization, Mendaki, to be led by

Malay members of parliament. The group was to encourage educational progress, which in turn would increase the financial wellbeing of the community. Finally, perhaps most telling was what developed in the integrated housing units. Once people had greater choice about where to live, communities began to resegregate. In studies regarding people's likes and dislikes about government housing, one of the frequent complaints was lack of community, little neighborliness, and other indicators of a sense of communal isolation. There developed certain areas where members of a particular ethnic community tended to live in greater number.

Changes in the housing situation facilitated this partial resegregation. By 1989, the Housing Development Board had built well over 800,000 apartments and virtually the entire population had adequate housing.[23] The Board permitted people to purchase their apartments at affordable costs, and by the mid-1980s, the vast majority of people owned their own homes in the apartment blocks. Workers used their contributions to the Central Provident Fund for housing purchases, thus the increase in homeownership did not reduce the government's role in people's lives. Instead, the government essentially became banker to most citizens, especially considering that most people did their personal banking at the Post Office Savings Bank, a government operation. The buying and selling of homes permitted people greater choice in where they lived, and thereby undermined the policy of full ethnic integration in housing.

The social engineering plan with perhaps the greatest success was the Stop at Two program to halt population growth. Singapore achieved zero growth by the later part of the 1970s, and by the mid-1980s, the program had overshot its mark. Women were in the workforce in increasing numbers; and although a substantial wage gap existed, women actually had an advantage in employment and gaining seniority, since they did not have to serve in the military like their male counterparts. Women with higher earnings and women of the Chinese community tended to have the fewest children, whereas poor women and women of the Malay and Indian communities tended to have more, but the overall trend was sharply downward. Suddenly the government needed to engineer population growth, although it sought to do this selectively, encouraging poorer and less educated people to stop at two but encouraging wealthier and more educated women to have more. Policy makers put in place various incentives to promote reproduction, including tax rebates, medical and housing benefits, priority in school choice, and childcare assistance. The government also created a Social Development Unit that acted like a matchmaking service for university graduates. It sponsored weekend retreats with equal numbers of male and female attendees; there were lessons in table manners, dancing, and other social skills. Despite the effort, there was little success in halting the slide of the birthrate.

One problem of social development to which government gave no attention was an increasing gap between the haves and the have-nots. There were members of society, typically the wealthier ones, who were fully integrated into the globalized city that Singapore had become, working on international finance deals, working for multinational corporations, traveling overseas on business, etc. There was another part of society that had been left behind and was not living globalization. Tensions increased in the 1980s, although the government dismissed them as "politics of envy."

Political Developments

The PAP retained power throughout this period, although with some upsets. Having become accustomed to no opposition in the Parliament since 1966, it came as a shock in 1981 when a member of the Worker's Party won a seat in a special election. The situation grew more alarming in the 1984 general election when the PAP lost two seats to the opposition. While this did not compromise the PAP's ability to rule whatsoever, it was nevertheless a blow to party leaders. Lee Kwan Yew declared, "If . . . it continued this way then the one-man-one-vote system must lead to our decline, if not our disintegration."[24] To address an apparent desire for opposition voices, the government decided to add up to three nonvoting opposition members of parliament if opposition parties won fewer than three seats in an election. More to the point of protecting its power, prior to the next general election in 1988, the government enacted a significant change to the representation system in Parliament. Instead of having a single member of parliament represent voters in a given district (called constituency), the PAP began a process that continued over the years to shift to group representation constituencies in which a number of single member districts would be consolidated and represented by a group of parliamentarians. In the initial round in 1988, each of the group constituencies had three representatives, and one of the three had to be either Malay or Indian in order for the group representation system to meet the government's stated goal of increasing minority representation in Parliament. Opponents of the system criticized the move as an effort to prevent opposition parties from winning seats, as they have to win a majority of the vote in larger voting units. No party other than the PAP has won seats in a group representation constituency since the system started in 1988.

Beyond its engagement with the questions surrounding parliamentary elections, the PAP expanded government influence over political actors in other ways during this period, including new legislation to exert greater control over the media. The 1974 Newspaper and Printing Presses Act mandated newspaper companies, editors, and printers to obtain annually renewed licenses, which the government may choose not to renew; in 1977 most of the country's newspapers were brought under the control of a government holding company. In 1986, further legislation included provisions to restrict foreign publications that might influence Singaporean public opinion; the *Far Eastern Economic Review* and *Wall Street Journal Asia*, both highly respected media organizations, fell afoul of these laws and had their issues confiscated and their reporters declared unwelcome in Singapore. In 1982, a prominent bureaucrat, S. R. Nathan (who became president of Singapore in 1999), was placed in charge of the leading English newspaper, the *Straits Times*. Under his leadership, other Singaporean newspapers were restructured and put under the authority of the *Straits Times*, leaving print journalism virtually under government control.

The colonial-era security laws continued to be harshly applied. Government officials used the Societies Act, created to restrict the Chinese secret societies a century earlier, to target the Roman Catholic Church, which had advocated on behalf of immigrant workers, in particular Filipino maids, some of whom faced physical and sexual abuse by their employers. These immigrant workers' few rights were largely unknown to them. When the Church sought to intervene on their behalf, the government expelled non-Singaporean priests and told the local Church organization to stay away from labor issues. The Internal Security Act continued to be a tool of authority, and legislators expanded its scope and frequency of use. In one notorious case, security officials detained Chia Thye Poh for 23 years on two-year renewable detention orders, which can be levied against anyone seen as a threat to security or the public order. Police arrested him in 1966 and did not release him until 1989, and then it was to a remote government house where he was prohibited from having any political visitors. People detained during this time period reported various forms of physical and psychological abuse, including beatings, sleep deprivation, threats to family, and forced confessions. Political leaders further strengthened the Act to permit any police officer to arrest a person believed to be a potential threat to security or social order, without a warrant, and hold that person for interrogation for up to 30 days.

Finally, another major tool for dealing with opponents is lawsuits for libel and defamation, in which Singaporean courts reliably rule in favor of government officials. To foreign newspapers, it is a reminder to be conscientious about what they publish about Singapore. To local individuals and organizations, such as opposition political parties, the common outcome is bankruptcy, which curtails political activities and has motivated a number of Singaporeans to flee the country to live in exile.

While the world changed much during these years and many of the earlier threats against social order in Singapore disappeared, the government saw an ongoing need for a strongly guided economy, society, and political system. A communist takeover would have undermined Singapore's thriving capitalist society, but by the late 1980s, both China and the Soviet Union, the ideological leaders for international communist action, were reforming their own economic systems. Communism no longer posed a realistic threat. Nevertheless, the old-guard leaders seemed trapped by their life experiences of existential threat and acted accordingly. Economist Linda Y. C. Lim noted that Singapore's economic development during this time had been praised by both free-market advocates like Milton Friedman and those that favored government intervention such as John Kenneth Galbraith. In a sense, Singapore's approach to economic development offered something for everyone with robust, government-guided capitalism. However, Lim concluded, "Since independence, what has made Singapore successful is not the Invisible Hand of the free market, but rather the very Visible Hand, indeed the Long Arm, of the State."[25]

THE NEXT GENERATION, 1990 ONWARD

Lee Kwan Yew, Singapore's Founding Father, relinquished some of his day-to-day duties already in 1985, and in 1990, the PAP chose a new prime minister, Goh Chok Tong, to succeed him. Goh Chok Tong began his career as a civil servant and was tapped for upper management of the government-led shipping company, Neptune Orient Lines, before the PAP recruited him to Parliament and then the prime ministership. In 1991, the new prime minister and his team released their strategy statement, "The Next Lap," outlining their plans and priorities for a future of "continuity and change." The main idea was to build on the established foundations: increase funding for education to promote economic growth, expand the labor force by increasing the population via immigration and larger family size, and help people be self-sufficient to avoid the perils of welfare-state-based government spending on social programs. In many respects there was little change: The economic plan established after the 1985 recession rolled along and the economy grew; the Housing Development Board shifted its focus to upgrading housing; commercial ties with China expanded to full diplomatic ties; and the PAP remained in complete control of the government. Goh Chok Tong spoke of a more open society, and relaxed some censorship of nonpolitical media. Police used the Internal Security Act less frequently against critics, although the courts still meted out judgments favoring the government in libel and defamation lawsuits.

One policy shift was the 1991 decision to have a national ideology, something that Malaysia and Indonesia had also adopted years earlier. Leaders labeled Singapore's national ideology "Shared Values," and in many respects it was a reiteration of the earlier and largely unsuccessful Confucian Values campaign. The Shared Values statement was a simplistic distillation of some basic ideas from the cultures that comprised Singapore's citizenry. There were five points: nation before community and society above self; family as the basic unit of society; community support and respect for the individual; consensus, not conflict; and racial and religious harmony. These were to stand in contrast to the individualist values of Western democracies that were plagued by crime, divorce, welfare programs, and the eventual financial ruin of the country as governments spend more to feed the ever expanding needs of society to assure reelection. Critics suggested the Shared Values were, as with the Confucian Values, a justification for the government to maintain tight political control.

Another nominal policy shift involved the presidency. The idea had been discussed in the 1980s, but it was not until later that the government transformed the presidency from a ceremonial, appointed office to an elected office with limited powers of oversight to prevent corruption (such as nepotistic appointments to the civil service) or unwise spending of the national reserve. The first election took place in 1993, but subsequent elections have not occurred due to the lack of opposing candidates. The Presidential Elections Commission oversees candidate selection based on qualifications standards so stringent, it is estimated that only about 400 Singaporeans could meet the criteria.[26]

Indeed, through much of the 1990s, there was very little change, but late in the decade, a series of shocks brought about the worst recession since independence. It began in 1997 when the Asian Economic Crisis that started in Thailand spread to Indonesia, Malaysia, and beyond. Singapore's level of investment in these countries and the amounts of weakened currency held by the banks was enough to push Singapore's economy into recession. The government cut salaries for public employees, scaled back housing improvements, reduced employer contributions to the Central Provident Fund, and increased spending on programs such as education that would offer long-term economic benefits. The government also reassessed its strategy to cope with the increasingly rapid changes in the global economy. With the ascension of China and India and the improved development of other Southeast Asian countries, Singapore faced ever more competition. Leaders had to be vigilant about adjusting to meet new challenges and to capitalize on new opportunities. When economy began to recover in 2001, the government promoted alliances or mergers between Singaporean businesses and major global competitors in order to participate in the developing trend of consolidation within industries. For example, already in 2000, Singapore Airlines joined the Star Alliance, an international network of airlines that integrated their operations and shared passengers. Potential international partners pressured regulators for greater openness in business practices. At the same time, the World Trade Organization pushed for reduced regulation (liberalization) of sectors like finance and telecommunications. The government continued to encourage investment in poorer countries but began promoting investment in wealthy countries as well, such as SingTel's (Singapore's telecommunications company) purchase of a major part of the second biggest telecommunications company in Australia.

While the strategy was in place, Singapore confronted additional jolts that undermined the fledgling recovery from recession. The September 11, 2001 terrorist attack on the United States was a blow to the global economy, and caused a spike in national security concerns. As the wealthiest and only non-Muslim country in its neighborhood, the government feared Singapore might be a target for Muslim extremists, particularly those of Jemaah Islamiyah, an Indonesian-based terrorist group seeking the establishment of an Islamic state comprised of Indonesia, the southern Philippines, and the Malay Peninsula. Singapore increased its internal security provisions, resulting in the arrest of 15 Singaporeans in December 2001, and another 21 in September 2002, on charges of plotting terrorist attacks in Singapore and other countries. This spawned deep concern about how well the Malay population was integrated into Singaporean society. These events had economic repercussions, as did the outbreak of SARS (Severe Acute Respiratory Syndrome) in 2003, which killed 33 Singaporeans and caused a 30 percent drop in tourism.[27] In 2004, a tsunami devastated parts of Indonesia and Thailand, and harmed the region's economy. At about the same time, there was another global health scare with Avian Flu.

Singapore's integration into the global economy has and will present challenges for the government and people. Singapore's political leadership continues to push for changes that advance it as a knowledge-based economy to keep up with or ahead of the competition. Another political transition occurred in 2004, when Lee Hsien Loong, the son of Lee Kwan Yew, succeeded Goh Chok Tong as prime minister. Lee Hsien Loong has set his own path. Revised economic development plans target new areas of growth, some with significant political controversy. The most controversial involved the 2010 opening of two integrated resorts that offer casino gambling. While the government had long opposed gambling, the pragmatic new leadership concluded that it was too good an opportunity to pass up. The government hopes to increase tourism, which grew through the nineties but dropped off after 2001, and also capture some of the estimated billions that it is losing to Singaporeans going abroad to gamble. In typical fashion, however, controls limit the potential damage to Singaporeans. Citizens have to pay an admission of 100 Singaporean dollars per visit or 2,000 Singaporean dollars per year, whereas foreigners can enter for free.[28] Singaporeans may not gamble on credit, and the government expanded counseling and rehabilitation services to help cope with gambling-related problems. The government also seeks to make Singapore a global education hub by capitalizing on its recent heavy investments in higher education. The goal is to have 150,000 international students at Singaporean universities by 2015.[29] The third area for major development is medical tourism. Singapore offers first-rate medical care at minimal cost compared to the high costs of healthcare in the United States. For example, the 2006–07 cost of a heart bypass surgery in the United States was 130,000 U.S. dollars, whereas in Singapore it could be done for 18,500 U.S. dollars. The government's target is one million medical tourists by 2012.[30]

Still, challenges remain. Efforts to improve the birth rate have thus far failed, but the government keeps trying. The government now offers a Baby Bonus for second and third children, and a baby fund to which the government will deposit yearly matching funds to parental contributions for second and third children. More recently, the government announced a bigger bonus of 10,000 Singaporean dollars for third and fourth children.[31]

As is common for highly globalized, knowledge-based economies, there are growing concerns and tensions that less-educated people are being left behind. At the same time as the bottom 20 percent of families suffered a decrease in income, Singapore was revealed to have had the greatest increase (22.4%) in number of millionaires among 68 countries studied.[32] The government keeps pushing for family responsibility, and has mandated that children must care for their elderly parents, but the new reality Singapore faces is structural unemployment, a form of unemployment caused by the nature of the global economy that is difficult to overcome. Thus, the wealth gap will likely continue and perhaps increase, possibly causing greater discontent.

How Singapore handles these problems will determine how the country changes in the future. Singapore's globalization thus far has been intensive in the economic and social sectors, but political globalization, which includes characteristics like expanded democracy, has been more limited. Singapore's second generation of leaders does not appear substantially different from the first. Both have demonstrated a pragmatic approach to continue economic growth and justify their continuing political leadership. However, this may become more difficult as the economic competition becomes sharper, as dissatisfaction by those not participating in the economy grows, and as the government's control of the media, especially the Internet, becomes weaker. Thus far, Singapore's government has been relatively successful at limiting political criticism on the Internet, but this may not continue, since the country has extensive Internet penetration. Can the economy grow forever and will the people continue to be satisfied with wealth but not meaningful political participation? The People's Action Party hopes so.

NOTES

1. Tilak Abeysinghe, "Singapore: Economy," in *The Far East and Australasia*, 39th ed., edited by Lynn Daniel (London: Europa Publications, Routledge, 2008), http://courses.nus.edu.sg/course/ecstabey/Singapore%20Economy-Tilak.pdf.

2. C. M. Turnbull, *A History of Singapore, 1819-1988*, 2nd ed. (New York: Oxford University Press, 1989), 312.

3. Malcolm Murfett et al., *Between Two Oceans* (New York: Marshall Cavendish International, 2004), 400.

4. C. M. Turnbull, *A History of Singapore*, 294.

5. Ibid., 296.

6. Ibid., 295.

7. Linda Y. C. Lim, "Singapore's Success: The Myth of the Free Market Economy," *Asian Survey* 23 (1983), 752–763, 753.

8. C. M. Turnbull, *A History of Singapore*, 293.

9. Ibid., 296.

10. Carl A. Trocki, *Singapore: Wealth, Power and the Culture of Control* (New York: Routledge, 2006), 163.

11. Singapore Elections, "Singapore Parliamentary General Election 1972," Singapore-Elections.Com, http://www.singapore-elections.com/parl-1972-ge/.

12. Quoted in Melanie Chew, "Human Rights in Singapore: Perceptions and Problems," *Asian Survey* 34 (1994), 933–948, 941.

13. Quoted in Neil A. Englehart, "Rights and Culture in the Asian Values Argument: The Rise and Fall of Confucian Ethics in Singapore," *Human Rights Quarterly* 22 (2000), 548–568, 551.

14. Kishore Mahbubani, "The Dangers of Decadence: What the Rest Can Teach the West," *Foreign Affairs* 72 (1993), 10–14.

15. Quoted in Neil A. Englehart, "Rights and Culture in the Asian Values Argument: The Rise and Fall of Confucian Ethics in Singapore," *Human Rights Quarterly* 22 (2000), 548–568, 553.

16. Quoted in C. M. Turnbull, *A History of Singapore*, 298–299.

17. Quoted in Neil A. Englehart, "Rights and Culture in the Asian Values Argument: The Rise and Fall of Confucian Ethics in Singapore," *Human Rights Quarterly* 22 (2000), 548–568, 554.

18. C. M. Turnbull, *A History of Singapore*, 312–313.

19. Carl A. Trocki, *Singapore: Wealth, Power and the Culture of Control*, 168.

20. Ibid., 167.

21. Teck-Wong Soon and William A. Stoever, "Foreign Investment and Economic Development in Singapore: A Policy-Oriented Approach," *The Journal of Developing Areas* 30 (1996), 317–340, 330.

22. Quoted in Neil A. Englehart, "Rights and Culture in the Asian Values Argument: The Rise and Fall of Confucian Ethics in Singapore," *Human Rights Quarterly* 22 (2000), 548–568, 555.

23. Carl A. Trocki, *Singapore: Wealth, Power and the Culture of Control*, 144.

24. C. M. Turnbull, *A History of Singapore*, 319–320.

25. Linda Y. C. Lim, "Singapore's Success: The Myth of the Free Market Economy," *Asian Survey* 23 (1983), 752–763, 758.

26. Terence Chong, "Singapore: Globalizing on Its Own Terms," in *Southeast Asian Affairs 2006*, ed. Daljit Singh and Lorraine Carlos Salazar (Singapore: Institute of Southeast Asian Studies, 2006), 278.

27. Carl A. Trocki, *Singapore: Wealth, Power and the Culture of Control*, 177.

28. Terence Chong, "Singapore: Globalizing on Its Own Terms," 271–272.

29. Tilak Abeysinghe, "Singapore: Economy," 7.

30. Ibid., 7.

31. Ibid., 9–10.

32. Terence Chong, "Singapore: Globalizing on Its Own Terms," 269.

Notable People in the History of Singapore

Crawfurd, Dr. John (1783–1868). He was the third resident (chief administrator) of Singapore, taking over from Raffles in 1823 and serving until 1826. He assisted in negotiating Singapore's final status with the Malay nobility in Singapore in 1824. He also affirmed Singapore's status as a free-trade port.

Churchill, Sir Winston (1874–1965). He was the prime minister of Great Britain during World War II, making many decisions that shaped Singapore's fate during that war.

Farquhar, Col. William (1770–1839). He assisted Raffles in founding the colony and served as the first resident/chief administrator from 1819 to 1822. He left an enduring mark on Singapore in establishing it as a free-trade port, and inviting much of its early immigration from the Malay Peninsula. He was significant in holding the colony secure in its first years.

Fong Swee Suan (1931–). He was one of Singapore's leading labor and student organizers in the 1950s and 1960s and promoted anticolonial activities. He was a member of the People's Action Party, but was in the radical, communist branch blamed for much political unrest. He was jailed repeatedly for inciting unrest, including as result of Operation Cold Store in 1963. After being released from prison, he settled in Malaysia and had a career in business.

Goh Chok Tong (1941–). He was the second prime minister of the Republic of Singapore from 1990 to 2004, taking over after Lee Kwan Yew's retirement. He began his career in administrative service, and then was in management of a government-led shipping company before being recruited into politics for the People's Action Party. He was the first prime minister from the second generation of leaders and remains active in the cabinet of his successor, Lee Hsien Loong, son of Lee Kwan Yew.

Goh Keng Swee (1918–2010). He was the economic architect of modern Singapore, having served as Minister of Finance and of Defense and as chair of the Monetary Authority and several government-led companies. He was very much in the People's Action Party inner circle, designing key policies that shaped the economic development and industrialization of Singapore as well as making the country a center for finance.

Hussein (–1835). He was the Sultan of Johor-Riau who signed the treaty with Raffles granting the English East India Company permission to establish a trading settlement in Singapore. He gained the title of sultan from a half-brother through the Company's acknowledgement of his status in return for the treaty.

Lee Kwan Yew (1923–). He was the first prime minister of Singapore and served as chief minister prior to that, holding the top executive position from 1959 to 1990. He founded the People's Action Party, Singapore's dominant political party, negotiated merger with Malaysia, and then led Singapore through the collapse of the merger and on to independence. He is the father of modern Singapore and fundamentally shaped the direction the country took after independence. He continued to serve after his retirement as minister mentor, advising the two prime ministers who have followed him.

Lim Chin Siong (1933–1996). He was a communist labor and student union organizer and a founder of the People's Action Party. He served in the Legislative Assembly and led the communist wing of the party, opposing British imperialism, until a group of disaffected party members broke away in 1961, forming the opposition party, Barisan Sosialis. He was jailed for six years due to the violent nature of some of his political activities and spent some time in London in exile, before returning to Singapore in 1979 where he lived until his death.

Lim Yew Hock (1914–1984). He was the second chief minister of Singapore, serving from 1956–1959. He was involved with the labor movement prior to entering politics with the Singapore Progressive Party. He was later a leader in the Labour Front, and it was with this party that he became chief minister, with his most notable accomplishments being the negotiation of Singapore's self-government and opposition to communist political action. He left politics in 1963 after his party, the People's Alliance Party, failed to win any seats in the 1963 election. He became a citizen of Malaysia and worked for the Malay government for several years.

Marshall, David Saul (1908–1995). He was the first chief minister once Singapore began its process toward self-governance, serving from 1955–1956. He was a lawyer and community activist and joined the Singapore Progressive Party for a time before becoming disaffected and founding the Labour Front. He became chief minister in Singapore's first election for the Legislative Assembly. He struggled to make the British governor take the new, elected government seriously, and eventually succeeded. He resigned as chief minister after failing to negotiate further steps toward self-governance, yet most of his goals were realized by the subsequent administration. He returned to politics and founded the Workers' Party.

Mountbattan, Lord Louis (1900–1979). He was the British naval officer who, as Supreme Allied Commander, Southeast Asia, oversaw the Japanese surrender of Singapore following World War II. He was also in charge of the British Military Administration reconstruction efforts immediately after the war. Despite corruption in the lower levels undermining the Administration's authority with the people, significant achievements were made in rebuilding the infrastructure, including the port, reopening schools, and reforming the police in the months immediately after the end of the war.

Parmeswara (–1411). He was the fifth ruler of ancient Singapore from approximately 1391–1397, until he was driven out and moved the Singapore settlement to Melaka.

Pervical, Gen. Arthur E. (1887–1966). He was the British Lieutenant-General in charge of ground forces during the attempt to defend the Malay Peninsula and Singapore from the Japanese invasion in 1941. He surrendered to the Japanese in Singapore on February 15, 1942, and spent the rest of the conflict as a prisoner of war in Singapore and other locations before returning to Britain after the war. He has received considerable blame for the fall of Singapore, although most recognize that it was a broad and multifaceted failure that was not solely Percival's fault.

Raffles, Sir Thomas Stamford (1781–1826). He is credited with founding Singapore and served as Singapore's second resident (chief administrator) for a short time in 1823. It was his insistence that Singapore became a free-trade port. He also marginalized the Malay nobility. He was a commoner but rose to be Lieutenant-Governor of the English East India Company's Bengkulu holdings. He retired from the Company in 1823.

Rajaratnam, Sinnathamby (1915–2006). He was Singapore's first and longest-serving foreign minister after independence, holding office from 1965 to 1980. He was a cofounder of the People's Action Party and a part of the inner circle who formed modern Singapore. As foreign minister, he played a key role in establishing relations with various countries that contributed to Singapore's security and economic development, which was tied very closely to foreign investment. He also pushed for Singapore to be included among the founding members of the Association of Southeast Asian Nations (ASEAN), an important international organization.

Sang Nila Utama. He was also known as Sri Tri Buana and was a prince from Palembang who founded the first known settlement at Singapore in 1299. He and his heirs, five rulers in all, established a capital at Singapore that stood until they were forced to relocate to Melaka in 1397 or 1398.

Sri Tri Buana. See Sang Nila Utama.

Temenggong Abdul Rahman (–1825). He was the Malay official who was based in Singapore prior to the arrival of Raffles and who brokered a deal giving the British access to Singapore in exchange for official recognition of his son-in-law Hussein as Sultan of Johor-Riau.

Tsuji, Col. Masanobu (1902–1961?). He was the Japanese colonel in charge of planning the invasion of the Malay Peninsula and Singapore. Well-known for his brutality, he is blamed for the massacre of tens of thousands of Chinese Singaporeans in the early days of the Japanese occupation in 1942. Following the war, he disappeared into China and remained there until the British closed the file on his potential prosecution for war crimes. He returned to Japan, wrote a book about his wartime experiences, and was elected to the Japanese parliament. He was last seen in Laos in 1961; and it is assumed that he was killed that year, although he was not legally declared dead until 1968.

Yamashita, Gen. Tomoyuki (1885–1946). He was the Japanese Imperial Army general who commanded the invasion of the Malay Peninsula and Singapore in 1941. He was nicknamed the "Tiger of Malaya" for his rapid sweep down the Peninsula, taking Singapore in only 70 days, 30 days faster than the Japanese anticipated. At the end of the war, he surrendered to American forces in the Philippines, where he was tried for war crimes and executed.

Glossary

Bang: A group within the Singaporean Chinese community whose membership was based on Chinese dialect group and region of origin in China. There were five main *bangs*: Cantonese, Hainanese, Hakka, Hokkien, and Teochew.

Bendahara: A noble title in the Malay court, this official was ranked second behind the sultan and is approximately equivalent to a prime minister.

British Commonwealth: An organization of Britain and a number of its former colonies, who work cooperatively and have formal allegiance to the British Crown.

Bugis: A seafaring people of the region who were key players in Malay court politics and traders throughout the islands of Indonesia and Singapore.

Chinese Protectorate: A colonial government office created to address abuses of unskilled Chinese workers.

Entrepôt Port: A transshipment port where goods are brought in from one location, traded, and then sent to another location—very few trade goods are of local origin.

Export-Led Industrialization: An economic development model that promotes the creation of industry though producing exportable items, often funded by foreign investment. This has become a dominant economic development model in recent decades.

Globalization: The process of countries and peoples growing more integrated and economically, politically, and socially interconnected.

Guomindang: The Nationalist Party in China, which had many supporters among the Singaporean Chinese community. After the 1949 Chinese Communist Revolution, the leaders fled to Taiwan and established a government on the island.

Import-Substitution Industrialization: A model of economic development that calls for poor countries to put up barriers to imported products and instead to build new domestic industries to produce goods to replace the foreign imports, and thereby jumpstart the industrial growth of a country. This was a leading economic development model in the 1960s.

Indentured Workers: The majority of migrant workers who settled in Singapore from China and some from India. Under indenture, workers have to pay back the cost of their transportation, labor recruitment costs, and other expenses, often at inflated prices, before they are able to choose where they work.

Konfrontasi: Translated as *confrontation*, this was an undeclared war from 1963–1966 waged by Indonesia against Malaysia and Singapore to disrupt the merger between the two territories.

Malay Annals: A semi-mythological history of the Malay nobility, whose roots were in Singapore. Passed down by oral tradition, it was finally written in the fifteenth century.

Orang Laut: Various peoples comprising a group of sea nomads. During times of political organization in Southeast Asia, these groups often served the local sultan as a naval defense force; however, in times of weak political authority, these peoples instead acted as pirates.

Revenue Farms: Strictly-regulated government monopolies of opium and liquor that were auctioned to private interests by the government as a source of revenue. The government would then charge rent on the farms as a source of ongoing income.

Secret Societies: Secretive groups found in the Singaporean Chinese community. They provided benefits, in particular, to newly arrived immigrants from China but were also involved in considerable social unrest and were ultimately banned by the government.

Sook Ching: The "purification by purging" that Japanese occupation forces undertook against the Chinese community with the goal of removing anyone who the Japanese thought was untrustworthy. In fact, the process was very indiscriminate and cost the lives of as many as 50,000 people.

Straits-Chinese: A term referring to persons of Chinese ethnicity who were born in the Straits Settlements, rather than being born in China and immigrating to Singapore.

Straits Settlements: A term referring to the unified British holdings on the Malay Peninsula of Penang, Melaka, and Singapore. The Straits Settlements were created in 1826 after the Dutch agreed to leave the British alone to establish a sphere of influence based on the Malay Peninsula. The Straits Settlements were directly administered from Kolkata by the English East India Company and later by the Colonial Office in London.

*Temenggong***:** A noble title in the Malay court, this official was ranked third behind the sultan and is approximately equivalent to a minister of justice and defense.

Bibliographic Essay

For a work spanning Singapore's history since the British colonization, one should turn to C. M. Turnbull's *A History of Modern Singapore* (Singapore: NUS Press, 2009). The emphasis in this very detailed volume tends toward administrative and political matters, but it does not neglect economic and social developments. Malcolm Murfett, John N. Miksic, Brian P. Farrell, and Chiang Ming Shun offer a very comprehensive military history in *Between To Oceans: A Military History of Singapore from First Settlement to Final British Withdrawal* (Singapore: Times Academic Press, 1999). This volume gives an especially helpful overview of the pre-British era, one that is otherwise relatively difficult to access in depth outside of specialized collections. However, it would be challenging for those readers of the World War II era who are unfamiliar with British military history as the text becomes encumbered by acronyms and detail. Finally, Carl A. Trocki's *Singapore: Wealth, Power and the Culture of Control* (New York: Routledge, 2006) makes a provocative argument about the trajectory of societal control, for which contemporary Singapore is well known, from the colonial period to independent Singapore. In addition to this volume, Trocki has written several other noteworthy additions to the literature on Singapore, including *Price of Pirates: The Temenggongs and the Development of Johor and Singapore 1784–1885, 2nd ed.* (Singapore:

NUS Press, 2007), *Opium and Empire: Chinese Society in Colonial Singapore 1800–1910* (Ithaca: Cornell University Press, 1990), and *Paths Not Taken: Political Pluralism in Post-War Singapore* (co-authored with Michael Barr) (Honolulu: University of Hawaii Press, 2009).

If one seeks a more contextual examination of Singapore, one may wish to examine *Contemporary Southeast Asia*, edited by Mark Beeson (New York: Palgrave Macmillan) This volume offers comparative examinations of Singapore and its neighbors on topics ranging from colonization and decolonization, economy, democratization, ethnicity and nationalism, international relations, and environmental issues.

For those especially interested in World War II, journalist Peter Elphick offers a detailed, yet approachable account in *Singapore: The Pregnable Fortress* (London: Hodder and Stoughton, 1995), a volume that caused political backlash in Australia. For a more scholarly examination, one does well to look at Karl Hack and Kevin Blackburn's *Did Singapore Have to Fall? Churchill and the Impregnable Fortress* (New York: Routledge Curzon, 2004), which examines answers to that question from various writers and then seeks to sort out the facts.

Those interested in the Singaporean Indian community or the dynamics of one of Singapore's ethnic neighborhoods are invited to read *Singapore's Little India: Past, Present, and Future*, 2nd ed. by Sharon Siddique and Nirmala Shotam (Singapore: Institute of Southeast Asian Studies, 1984). This small volume helps the community come alive with maps, drawings, and old and new photographs, as well as a detailed narrative.

Two noteworthy volumes that must be mentioned are from a couple of Singapore's most influential political leaders. Lee Kwan Yew's auto-biography, *From Third World to First: The Singapore Story 1965-2000* (New York: HarperCollins, 2000) is lengthy and can be a little difficult at times for those without any background in economics, but it is undeniably interesting to hear about Singapore's recent decades from the man who was behind many of the events. An interesting partner to this volume is Goh Keng Swee's *The Economics of Modernization* (Singapore: Marshall Cavendish Academic, 2004). Goh was the architect of Singapore's economic development plan and has much to offer. The volume is a collection of speeches on various topics and is approachable in its level of difficulty. The greatest problem may be finding an affordable copy outside of Singapore; it is suggested to seek it in a library. For those desiring a shorter and narrower discussion of Singapore's economic development model, read "Foreign Investment and Economic Development in Singapore" by Teck-Wong Soon and

William A. Stoever in the *Journal of Developing Areas* (Vol. 30, No. 3, April 1996, p. 317–340).

Since most of the visible evidence of Singapore's history has disappeared in the face of economic development, an examination of Gretchen Liu's *Singapore: A Pictorial History 1819–2000* (Singapore: Didier Millet, 2007) may be a welcome addition to readers. This volume has over 1,000 photographs and drawings covering each of the ethnic groups and a range of topics.

Finally, it would be remiss to omit an online resource offered by Singapore's National Library Board called *Singapore Infopedia* (http://infopedia.nl.sg/index.html). This searchable Web site offers a series of well-researched and well-documented short essays on major historical events, important figures, and culture, architecture, nature, etc. It is an excellent resource for basic information.

Index

About the Author

JEAN E. ABSHIRE is associate professor of political science and international studies and head of the Department of Political Science at Indiana University Southeast, New Albany, IN. Abshire has received two Fulbright grants to conduct international research, particularly in the areas of ethnicity and nationalism.

Other Titles in the Greenwood Histories of the Modern Nations
Frank W. Thackeray and John E. Findling, Series Editors

The History of Afghanistan
Meredith L. Runion

The History of Argentina
Daniel K. Lewis

The History of Australia
Frank G. Clarke

The History of the Baltic States
Kevin O'Connor

The History of Brazil
Robert M. Levine

The History of Bulgaria
Frederick B. Chary

The History of Cambodia
Justin Corfield

The History of Canada
Scott W. See

The History of Central America
Thomas Pearcy

The History of the Central
Asian Republics
Peter L. Roudik

The History of Chile
John L. Rector

The History of China,
Second Edition
David Curtis Wright

The History of Congo
Didier Gondola

The History of Cuba
Clifford L. Staten

The History of the Czech
Republic and Slovakia
William M. Mahoney

The History of Egypt
Glenn E. Perry

The History of El Salvador
Christopher M. White

The History of Ethiopia
Saheed Adejumobi

The History of Finland
Jason Lavery

The History of France
W. Scott Haine

The History of Germany
Eleanor L. Turk

The History of Ghana
Roger S. Gocking

The History of Great Britain
Anne Baltz Rodrick

The History of Greece
Elaine Thomopoulos

The History of Haiti
Steeve Coupeau

The History of Holland
Mark T. Hooker

The History of India
John McLeod

The History of Indonesia
Steven Drakeley